MW00709448

Run, Amy, Run!

Beth Huffman

May you be touched by Amy's inspirational life.

Beth Huffman

STANLEY PUBLISHING CO.

Run, Amy, Run!
Copyright ©2010 by Beth Huffman

All rights reserved. No part of this book may be used or reproduced in any manner whatsoever or by any electronic or mechanical means including information storage and retrieval systems without written consent from the publisher, except for brief quotations for reviews.

Original edition published in the United States by Stanley Publishing Company.
El Paso, Tx
www.stanleypublishing.com

Huffman, Beth
Run, Amy, Run!
ISBN 978-0-615-55295-8

First Printing 2011

Cover design by Rishi Arora
www.rishinealarora.com

Book design by Marsha Morris

Printed in the United States

Acknowledgements

Amy Greer's life was defined by her loving heart and courageous spirit. She was a valiant warrior who battled cystic fibrosis, the disease that seized control of her life and every breath she took.

Amy had hoped to write her own story but ran out of time. Her dream was to share her journey and encourage others struggling with cystic fibrosis to have faith, to never give up and to embrace life.

Amy was passionate in wanting to raise public awareness for cystic fibrosis research. She was also passionate about encouraging people to sign their organ donor cards. Some caring donor gave Amy new lungs, a gift that enabled her to spend many more years with those she loved.

Many thanks go to Amy's family and friends who shared so much in writing her story Many thanks also go to the people from the Cystic Fibrosis Foundation for granting permission to cite medical information from their cff.org website. Finally, we'd like to thank Lifetouch National School Studios for permission to use Amy's photograph.

For Amy

Preface

Since 1955, the Cystic Fibrosis Foundation has been the driving force behind the pursuit of a cure for cystic fibrosis (CF), a genetic and chronic disease that affects the lungs and digestive system of about 30,000 children and adults in the United States. An additional ten million more – or about one in every 31 Americans—are carriers of the defective CF gene, but do not have the disease.

This defective gene and its protein product causes the body to produce unusually thick, sticky mucus to build up and clog some of the organs in the body, particularly the lungs and pancreas. When mucus clogs the lungs, it can make breathing very difficult. The thick mucus also causes bacteria to get stuck in the airways, which causes inflammation and life-threatening infections, as well as lung damage.

Mucus can also block the digestive tract and pancreas. The mucus stops digestive enzymes from getting to the intestines. The body needs these enzymes to break down food. People with cystic fibrosis often need to replace these enzymes with medicines they take with their meals and snacks, which help them digest food and get proper nutrition.

In order for people to have cystic fibrosis, they must inherit two copies of the defective CF gene – one copy from each parent. If both parents are carriers of the CF gene, their child will have a 25% chance of inheriting both defective copies and having cystic fibrosis, a 50% chance of inheriting one defective copy and being a carrier, and a 25% chance of not having CF or carrying the gene.

Cystic fibrosis is most common in Caucasians, but it can affect all races. The severity of symptoms is different from person to person. The most common symptoms are:
- Very salty-tasting skin
- Persistent coughing, at times producing phlegm
- Frequent lung infections, like pneumonia or bronchitis

- Wheezing or shortness of breath
- Poor growth/weight gain in spite of a good appetite
- Small, fleshy growths in the nose called nasal polyps
- Frequent greasy, bulky stools or difficulty in bowel movements

Most people are diagnosed with CF at birth through newborn screenings, or before the age of two-years old. A doctor who sees the symptoms of CF will order a sweat test or genetic test to confirm the diagnosis. A sweat test is the most common test used to diagnose cystic fibrosis and is considered the diagnostic 'gold standard.' A small electrode is placed on the skin (usually the arm) to stimulate the sweat glands. Sweat is then collected and the amount of chloride, a component of salt in the sweat, is measured. A high level of chloride means that the person has cystic fibrosis.

Currently, there is no cure for cystic fibrosis. However, specialized medical care, aggressive drug treatments and therapies, along with proper CF nutrition, can lengthen and improve the quality of life for those with CF.

In 1955, children with CF were not expected to live long enough to attend grade school. Today, thanks to continued Foundation-supported research and specialized care, an increasing number of people with CF are living into adulthood and leading healthier lives that include careers, marriages and families of their own.

Cystic fibrosis research is a team effort. Scientists across the world are working to understand and beat this complex disease, with the hope that one or more of the many approaches to therapies will lead to a cure.

Breathless

On a humid May morning in 1975, I pulled into the elementary school parking lot and was greeted by the sounds of young laughter from children at recess. Two girls were competing in a race, and the students were jumping up and down shouting, "Run, Amy, run!"

The pulsating cheers were for a slender girl who was running with all her might. It appeared this young competitor would win until she stopped abruptly in the middle of the race. As the girl desperately leaned over to catch her breath, two classmates quickly ran to her, put their arms around her waist, and steadied her as she gasped for air. Within moments, the girl regained her breath, stood up, and threw her arms around each friend's shoulder as they crossed the finish line together.

The school bell rang, and everyone reluctantly left the playground. As I followed the students, I asked a boy ahead of me if the girl who stopped running was sick.

"No, she's okay," he said with certainty. "That's just Amy. She can't breathe so good when she runs too fast."

Upon entering the building, I met my teaching colleague; we were sharing a ride to a county meeting for language arts teachers in grades K-12. I looked forward to telling her about the young girl in the race. There was something about this brave competitor. She left an indelible imprint in my mind that I couldn't verbalize. It was a feeling I would never forget.

When I learned the girl's name was Amy Core, I felt like I knew her somehow. Three of Amy's older siblings were in my high school English, speech and drama classes. Even though the siblings possessed distinctly different personalities, a family connection prevailed. They worked hard, never complained and reflected their parents' values. They wore their last name 'Core' like a badge of honor.

Amy made that morning unforgettable. Five years later, she

1

would be sitting in my 7th grade language arts class. Little did I know that she would teach me far more about the gift of life than could be found in any textbook.

Penny Loafers

As you drive east on a township road outside of Rawson, Ohio, on an early July evening, healthy fields of corn and beans embrace you. Silhouetted against the summer sky are towering concrete silos, the passionate symbols of a farm operation run by a man who was proud to be a farmer.

The modest, well-kept farmhouse across the road is where Bob and Leona Core raised their five children. Farming was more than a job to Bob. It was a chosen way of life, a reflection of the respect he had for his father and grandfather who had been farmers.

Bob and his siblings, Delores and Tom, were born at home and lived on a farm outside of Pandora, Ohio. Bob's work ethic was defined on this farm, where he milked cows by hand at 5 a.m. each day before going to school. This is the farm where his natural skills were cultivated when his father taught him how to work the fertile ground in preparation for spring planting.

When Bob was a teenager, his family moved to a farm near Findlay, Ohio, where his father bought 210 acres of ground. In addition to helping with the farming, Bob and Tom took on further responsibilities in raising livestock, which Bob especially enjoyed. Following high school graduation, he enrolled at Ohio State University to enter the agriculture veterinary program.

Without question, Bob was a country boy who didn't like city living. When he discovered that he needed to have the right contacts to get into the veterinary program, he became disillusioned. After attending college for nine months, he quit school and returned home. A few months later, he enlisted in the Navy.

Bob's time spent in the service was a daily reminder of how much he missed his family. Each time he came home to visit once a year, he found it that much harder to leave. At the end of his four years of military service, he was stationed in San Diego. Rather than drive home alone from California to Ohio, Bob's father decided the entire family would fly to San Diego and ride back with him. In order to afford four airline tickets, Bob's father sold ten of his dairy cows. This was a decision he never regretted. Everyone enjoyed the memorable trip and appreciated being together as a family again. Coming home had never looked so good.

Leona, the youngest of six children, was raised by her parents on a farm outside Rawson, Ohio. In addition to farming, her father provided for his family by painting buildings. When tires and rubber products were in demand during World War II, he also worked at Cooper Tire and Rubber in Findlay.

While Bob was serving in the Navy, Leona, who was seven years younger, was attending high school and working on the farm with her brothers and sisters. Following high school graduation, she was hired as a secretary at Marathon Oil in Findlay, where she enjoyed dating a young man from the area.

When Bob and Leona actually met is hard to say. They had known one another for years because their families both attended Powell Memorial United Methodist Church near Findlay. When Bob and Leona fell in love is not hard to say.

Upon returning home from the service, Bob quickly became aware of Leona's beauty. When he saw her at the Hancock County Fair, he worked his masculine charm and offered her two shiny pennies for her penny loafers. The romantic pursuit didn't end there. Bob knew Leona enjoyed dancing, so he wooed her further on Sunday evenings when they went square dancing.

Leona's boyfriend wasn't the least bit impressed with this older guy stealing his girl. In desperation, the boyfriend sought help from Leona's sister, Helen. The young man begged Helen to convince Leona to stop seeing the relentless Bob Core. The efforts were in vain. Helen told the young man that Leona was old enough to make up her own mind.

Leona did just that. She made up her mind and followed her heart. On August 5, 1956, Leona and Bob became husband and wife.

The Narrow Bridge

Leona told Bob she wanted boys when they decided to start their family, and it was no secret how happy Bob would have been to have sons to help with the farming. In the first six years of their marriage, Bob and Leona had four children whose names were Deb, Cathy, Lisa and Jill.

Six years after Jill was born, Leona was surprised to learn she was pregnant with their fifth child. The family doctor told Bob he was certain this baby would be a boy. Bob, who was known to enjoy dickering with people to get a good deal, challenged the doctor with a bet. If the baby were a boy, Bob would supply the doctor with free beef. If the baby were a girl, the doctor would provide a free delivery. Feeling confident, the doctor agreed to the bet. On November 29, 1968, Amy Jo Core was born and came into this world free of charge.

As Bob searched for farm ground to rent, he and Leona struggled financially in the early years of their marriage. Their first business decision as a married couple was to rent a farm near Findlay. When the owner later sold the acreage, Bob found ground to rent from another area landowner. When Deb was one year old, he moved his family to the farmhouse where all the girls were raised.

The family income was so limited one year that Bob took a second job at the local sugar beet plant in Findlay. Leona, who was an excellent seamstress, made her daughters' clothes, and that particularly lean year wrapped the girls' Christmas presents in newspaper. On Christmas morning, the girls were visibly disappointed with the wrapping paper, and Leona vowed she would never do that again, regardless of how little money the family had.

Bob didn't need sons to help run the farm because he had five daughters. The minute he thought his girls were old enough, they were bedding the cattle, unloading and stacking bales of straw

5

in the barn and picking up rocks from the fields. When Bob taught his daughters how to hoe the bean fields, he was clever in negotiating the price of field labor by paying five cents a row. It was a winning strategy. The girls were naively delighted to have an income, there were no weeds in the bean fields, and Bob didn't have to hire a sitter to watch his daughters when Leona went to her Ladies' Aide meetings at church. Amy was part of this cheap labor force, as long as it didn't interrupt playtime with her cat, Puffy, that she dressed in doll clothes and pushed around in a stroller.

Work on the farm wasn't limited to the fields. The five sisters painted everything from fences to barns and barn roofs. Bob believed if you were old enough to walk and talk, you could carry a paintbrush. Amy loved tagging along behind her sisters and carried her own paintbrush the day the five of them decided to get creative. They painted their names on the side of the barn and quickly painted over them before their dad returned to check their work. When Bob saw their artistry, he failed to appreciate the aesthetic beauty and yelled, "What are you doing painting your names on the barn!" (Actually, the girls recalled his language being a bit more colorful at the time). The girls didn't realize their names could easily be seen through the second coat of paint. This story had a happy ending for Bob. The side of the barn was repainted without any creative brush strokes.

The girls had responsibilities helping Leona, too. They were expected to help maintain a large garden and strawberry patch. As a result, they learned how to freeze and can the fruits and vegetables. When Leona was helping Bob with the farm work, they cooked the meals and did the dishes. Although they were too young to appreciate it, the girls had a wholesome upbringing. Bob raised cattle so they ate wonderful beef. Their fruits and vegetables were all homegrown and Leona made a delicious dessert with every meal. The girls thought store-bought cookies were a treat because theirs were always homemade.

Another treat for the girls was to take turns staying overnight at their grandparents' houses. This was a chance to get away from chores and to have fun with their cousins. Whenever there was an opportunity for harmless mischief growing up, Amy loved being part of it. At Grandma Core's house, Amy spent her time with Matt and Jay. One night, the three of them were horsing around in the house, which was always forbidden, and one of the boys threw a pillow that cracked a glass shade on the ceiling light. The trio agreed to tell their

6

grandma that Amy had done it because they knew she wouldn't get in trouble. When Amy explained what she had accidentally done, Grandma said, "Oh, Amy, it's okay. We can fix the shade. Don't worry about it." The day Grandma Core sold her house, the shade was still glued and the cousins still honored their secret pact.

As soon as the girls were tall enough to sit on a tractor seat, Bob taught them to hoe, rake, mow and disc the fields. Although they each had some memorable mishaps with the tractors, it was Amy who pulled off the most daring tractor feat, one that her father never could quite believe.

Bob continually stressed the importance of safety when his daughters were driving farm equipment. One afternoon, he made it clear to Amy what roads to take home with the rotary hoe she was pulling. Along the way, she got confused and improvised by taking a quicker route. When Amy returned home with all of the equipment intact, she was grinning proudly. Bob wasn't nearly as amused, especially when he learned she had driven across a bridge he knew was too narrow for the size of the equipment. At the very least, Amy should have wrecked, ripped off the rotary hoe or flipped the tractor when the equipment hit the bridge. Bob always swore that she must have been driving fast enough for the rotary hoe to hit a bump, causing it to bounce up and over the bridge abutments.

Strong-willed Bob saw the experience as a miracle. Strong-willed Amy saw it as an adventure. No one could have known that this strong-willed determination would become Amy's greatest ally in the years ahead when confronted with many life-threatening obstacles. No one could have known there would be many more narrow bridges for Amy to cross.

Amy's Battle Begins

When Amy was eight years old, her third grade teacher, Lorrie was concerned about Amy's frequent stomach pain, wheezing and coughing. Her concerns were intensified by the skin under Amy's fingernails that was thicker than average, causing a rounded or clubbed appearance. Lorrie had a close friend whose four-year-old daughter had cystic fibrosis, and Amy's physical symptoms were alarmingly similar.

Lorrie, who was a new teacher in the school system, agonized whether to call Leona and schedule a conference. As she envisioned how terribly distressing the conversation would be, Lorrie feared that she was invading the family's privacy. Although Lorrie hoped that her concerns were unfounded, her heart told her otherwise; she knew that she had to contact Amy's mother. Before making the phone call, Lorrie gathered medical literature on cystic fibrosis from her close friend.

Leona came to school immediately. As Lorrie cautiously started going over the information, Leona's facial expressions changed to visible anguish. With each symptom Lorrie described, Leona began to nod her head in despair and disbelief. At the end of the conference, they discussed having Amy examined by a pulmonary specialist.

Leona left the room blinded by tears. Lorrie carried the painful memories of that day in her heart for years to come. She thoroughly enjoyed having Amy in class and admired her incredible perseverance. If Amy did have cystic fibrosis, Lorrie feared that this horrific disease could one day destroy Amy's lungs.

Amy was tested immediately. Fear became reality when she was diagnosed with cystic fibrosis (CF), an inherited, chronic disease at birth, which affects the lungs and digestive system. A defective gene and its protein product cause the body to produce unusually thick, sticky mucus that clogs the lungs and leads to life-threatening lung infections. Bacteria can clog the airways that cause inflammation and infections that lead to lung damage. The mucus also obstructs the pancreas and stops natural enzymes from helping the body break down food and absorb nutrients.

To have CF, a person must inherit two copies of the defective CF gene-one copy from each parent. If both parents are carriers of the CF gene, (i.e. they each have one copy of the defective gene but do not have the disease themselves), their child will have a 25 percent chance of inheriting both defective copies and having CF, a 50 percent chance of inheriting one defective copy and being a carrier and a 25 percent chance of not having CF or carrying the gene.

Amy was given a sweat test, which is the most common test used to diagnose cystic fibrosis. A small electrode was placed on her arm to stimulate the sweat glands. The sweat was then collected and the amount of chloride, a component of salt in the sweat, was measured. A high level of chloride indicated that Amy had cystic fibrosis.

Amy had a variety of CF symptoms, which included very salty-tasting skin; persistent coughing, at times with phlegm; wheezing or shortness of breath; frequent lung infections like pneumonia or bronchitis; nasal polyps forming in the nose, and poor growth and weight gain in spite of a good appetite.

With the diagnosis, Amy's life had to change dramatically if she were to live. The Core family's life changed as well. When Bob and Leona explained Amy's health problems to her sisters, they recalled crying when they saw tears in their dad's eyes. Although they didn't understand the specifics of the disease, they knew it was serious. They knew Amy would need their help.

Deb understood the severity of the diagnosis more than her younger sisters. She knew a young lady from church who had recently passed away from CF at the age of 21. Deb also remembered the fear that raced through her body when one of the doctors said, "Cystic fibrosis will shorten Amy's life span."

Cathy was in her freshman year of college when Bob called to tell her about Amy's diagnosis. The dire tone in her father's voice said it all. Cathy remembered the many days when she and her sisters held their breath, waiting for Amy to stop coughing so hard and so long.

Amy was under the care of pulmonary specialists at Toledo Children's Hospital throughout the majority of her elementary, junior high and high school years. In order to help her digestive system, she immediately began taking enzyme tablets with meals that she called her 'food pills.' These tablets enabled her body to digest food more easily and were essential in helping provide proper food nutrition.

At least once a day, Amy used an aerosol inhaler, which created a mist made from liquid medicines that could reach her airways quickly. When she tried to avoid using it, due to the very bitter taste of the medications, Leona wouldn't allow it. Amy often cried because it was so depressing to repeat the same daily routine and still not feel well.

In order to breathe easier, Amy received daily breathing therapies called 'postural drainage and percussion treatments.' By watching physical therapists work on Amy, everyone in the family learned the procedure that used gravity and percussion to loosen the thick mucus in her lungs so it could be removed by coughing. Keeping the airways unclogged was critical to reducing the severity of lung infections.

Bob built a table made of steel and wood that was similar to those used at the hospital. The top was carpeted and could be adjusted to different horizontal angles. Amy would lie on the table, and one of her parents or sisters would cup each hand and start palpitating at the bottom of her spine. The palpating continued up her back and across her lobes. Amy then turned over and received chest palpitations. The therapy regimen was the same every day. When the girls got home from school, they did their homework, ate supper, helped with the dishes and gave Amy a treatment if it was their turn.

In the years ahead, Amy and Leona walked many miles up and down the country roads that surrounded their house. It was essential to Bob and Leona to treat Amy just like they did her sisters. Amy didn't want any pity or favoritism. Instead, she made a deliberate effort to live as normally as she could.

On October 9, 1978, Lisa wrote the following journal entry in response to an English assignment. The students were required to write a vivid description of an unforgettable moment spent with a loved one. Lisa chose to write about Amy.

I was helping Mom after supper. We were cleaning up and doing dishes when she asked me if I would run with Amy. I said, "Sure, as long as I don't have to do the dishes."

10

Mom agreed.

I put on my tennis shoes and went outside. Amy was hanging from the crossbar of the swing set. She was playing with a five-foot piece of garden hose when I said, "Get your buns in gear because I'm in better shape than you."

That was all it took to get Amy ready to run. We walked to the road and started running using the garden hose as a jump rope. When Amy started to tire, she held onto one end of the hose and I pulled her along. We stopped at the country bridge to catch our breath, look at the water and throw stones that we tried to make skip more than two times.

Once rested, I grabbed the hose and said, "Imagine this hose is a whip, and I'm in pursuit of a runaway tiger." I started chasing Amy and slapped the hose on the road to make a cracking sound and shouted, "Amy, halt in the name of Lisa!"

Amy ran about 200 feet from the bridge to the house nonstop. Eventually, we both sat down to catch our breath from the make-believe chase. I was exhausted. Like most kids, once you've got your older sister's attention, you work to keep it, so we played hide-and-go-seek with our dog, Tippy.

Amy was 9 and I was 17. It was great to play with my sister. I felt closer to her. It was the best feeling ever.

Two years later, Jill had the same writing assignment in English class. She chose to write about Amy.

Jo

She sits depressed as her teeth clench the mouthpiece.

Tears trickle down the unblemished face and drop helplessly onto her delicate hands, her frail silence.

The sound of her breathing is shut out only by the thunderous pounding of the cupped hands slapping her lower lobes.

The endless daily routine extending her life that she wants to be normal...finally.

It was never meant to be understood.

11

The New Friend

In 1979, Amy received the gift of friendship that would prosper throughout her adolescent, teenage and adult years. Amy would come to love this new friend like a sister. Karen, who had been living in Cincinnati, Ohio, moved into the school district when the girls were in fifth grade. Amy felt an immediate kinship with this new girl, whom she affectionately called her 'city slicker' friend.

Amy confided more about her disease to Karen than anyone outside her family. Consequently, Karen realized that Amy's lung problems were far more serious than people knew. During one of Amy's stays in the hospital, Karen felt honored when Amy said she could come visit her. That experience painted a lasting, vivid picture in Karen's mind when she saw how exhausted Amy was after her medical treatments. As she witnessed how hard Amy worked in her daily life to disguise her struggles, Karen realized even more that her best friend was a tenacious fighter.

One week when Amy was in the hospital, the junior high physical education teacher explained what cystic fibrosis was to Amy's classmates. The teacher was graphic in describing the damage that Amy's disease was doing to her lungs. There was a crippling silence when the teacher looked at everyone and said, "Amy will be lucky if she lives to graduate with you."

Karen was as shocked as her classmates. Amy had never told her this. They had talked about their dreams of getting married one day, having children and babysitting their grandchildren. Karen clearly remembered Amy saying that she was going to raise her kids just like she and her sisters were raised. She remembered the certainty in Amy's voice when she said, "I'm going to be the kind of mother that my mom is."

Suddenly, Karen was heartbroken and afraid for Amy. Their vow to be best friends for the rest of their lives took on a whole new meaning.

Another School Year

A new school year is about to begin. I will be teaching high school English, speech and drama classes in the morning and junior high language arts in the afternoon. I look forward to the challenges of each level, especially the junior high.

My high school students know the focus will be on writing. Each literature piece we read will be followed by a writing assignment. They also know they'll be required to keep a journal.

Keeping a journal will be a new concept to the junior high students. While the boys are rolling their eyes in boredom and disgust, I hope they hear me say, "You will get extra credit for your journal entries. They are an incentive to raise your grade. A journal can't hurt you, but it can definitely help you."

I've looked at my class rosters, and I'll have Amy Core in seventh grade. Her sisters have all graduated, so it's refreshing to know I'll still have one of the Core girls. I've read as much material as I can find on cystic fibrosis. The information is starkly grim. In order to live a long and healthy life, Amy will have to beat the medical odds. Somehow, I hope there are things I can do to make her bad days more bearable.

I've drawn up a seating chart and have her seated near the door, so she can quickly get a drink of water when she starts coughing. If the opportunity ever presents itself, I'm going to tell her about the day I saw her running in the race at recess. There will be no mention of her stopping to catch her breath. I just want her to know how much I admired her determination to win.

Amy's Journal

We've only been in school two weeks. Amy has already been in trouble twice in study hall for her constant talking. After school today, she flew into my room, dropped her cluttered notebook, and papers landed everywhere. There was nothing to do but laugh.

"Amy, you've got to be more organized."

"I know, Mrs. Huffman. My mom is always telling me to keep things picked up in my room. Believe it or not, my sister, Cathy is sloppier than I am. Then there's my sister, Lisa who is a neat freak. She actually likes to help Mom clean the house. That is totally dumb. Oh…did you hear? I've gotten in trouble twice in study hall."

I gave her a slight look of disapproval and said, "Yes, and I'm not too happy about it. The rules are the same for everyone. You can't keep pushing your luck, Amy."

"Yep. I know. That's why I wanted to ask you to write a pass for me to get out of study hall tomorrow. It's the same time as your conference period. No offense, Mrs. Huffman, but you need to change your bulletin boards. We are really tired of looking at the same posters. I could put up new ones. It will probably take all period. Then I won't get in trouble again. Please, get me out of there. I feel like I'm in prison."

"Okay. I'll write the pass for tomorrow. If you can finish the semester without getting in trouble again, I'll let you change my bulletin boards second semester. Do we have a deal?"

Amy grimaced and walked over to the calendar on the wall.

"How long is it until second semester starts?"

I turned the calendar pages and pointed to the date.

"Man, this is going to be tough, but I think I can do it. We have a deal. Let's shake on it."

"One more thing, Amy. You can't brag about getting out of study hall to anyone. You and I are the only two people who will know about this."

We shook hands and cemented the deal. As Amy started to leave the room, she said, "Can I just tell my mom and that's all?"

Knowing she would have the last word, I said, "Okay. Just your mom."

"Thanks, Mrs. Huffman. See you tomorrow."

"See you tomorrow, Amy."

I know I will be starting a journal tomorrow that will be exclusively about Amy. This free spirit is inspirational. In living with cystic fibrosis, she will be in a battle each day of her life. I have so much to learn from her.

The Bulletin Board Girl

Journal

September 1981

When Amy came to my room today, she had this ornery grin. It was obvious she enjoyed the secret deal we made. I was prepared to put her to work. Besides putting up new background paper for the bulletin boards, there were many posters she could choose. She loves cats, so it came as no surprise when she picked a poster of a lazy cat bemoaning the fact that he'd like mornings better if they started later in the day.

Amy got busy, and I started grading essays. Ten minutes into her work, she said, "Mrs. Huffman, am I allowed to talk while you're grading papers?"

"Sure. You talk and I'll listen."

"Is there anything special you want me to tell you? Do you want to hear about my friends or the cute boys in my class?"

"Why don't you tell me what it's like having four older sisters? Since I know them so well, it would be fun to hear your opinions."

Then Amy's narrative began. I turned over the attendance sheet and began to take notes of her thoughts, knowing this would be a journal entry I'd want to keep.

"Where do I even start? I could write a book about my sisters, especially Cathy since she always caught heck from Dad. When she was in high school, she never got home on time, and I mean never. She cracks me up. I've learned a lot of good tricks from her. I loved watching her in *Bye Bye Birdie*. When I take drama in high school, I hope you pick out a musical like that one because I want to do what she did. Cathy was great when she was singing. My dad never fell asleep and that's saying something. Did you know I'm a good

16

singer? All my sisters are. I know we didn't get it from the Core side of the family because my dad can't carry a tune in a bucket."

"Whenever my sisters and cousins say we have a lot of 'Core' in us, that means we're bull-headed. In Cathy's opinion, Dad is the most stubborn mule of all. I'm a lot like my dad because I have a temper, and I'm always looking for something to buy, if I can get a good deal on it. My dad's real tight with his money. I think that's a good thing. My dad works harder than anyone I know."

"I think Debbie is Dad's biggest helper with the farming. She loves to drive the tractor. She'll even haul manure. I'm not kidding. It doesn't bother her one bit. When you're a Core, it means you have to work. You don't have a choice. Debbie is a hard worker. Dad depends on her and Mom a lot to help him. The only time she makes me mad is when she tries to act like she's my mom and tells me what to do."

"Lisa tries to be like my mom sometimes, too. It's because they're older, I guess. I think Lisa is a lot like Mom because she's tenderhearted and cries at sad movies. She's definitely tall like my mom. You should see how clean Lisa keeps her bedroom. You'd never know we're sisters. When I was little, she'd play a game or mess around outside with me. I think she liked being with me most of the time. It was fun to watch her play basketball because she's usually a quiet person, so people thought she would act all nice in a game. No way! She's like Debbie. She hates to lose. That's what I mean about all of us Cores acting alike. We want to win, even if we have to lose our tempers and get mean."

"I see my sister, Jill, the most. She's closer to my age and is probably the most patient with me. We slept in the same bed. My dad barely heated our bedrooms, so when Jill got in bed in the winter, her feet were freezing when she rubbed them against mine. It felt good because I was always hot. I liked it when she told me stories about her friends and boyfriends."

"I definitely want you to pick out a play like *The Miracle Worker* when I'm in drama class. In my opinion, Jill was amazing. Sometimes, I forgot she was my sister because she acted just like Annie Sullivan. My favorite part of the play was at the end when she taught Helen Keller how to spell 'water.' My mom and I got tears in our eyes. My dad never cries, but I know he thought Jill was the best actress ever. So did I."

"I like all my sisters. It would be nice to have a brother, but

17

I wouldn't trade my sisters for one. Sometimes they tell me secrets, and I don't tell anyone. I think they trust me most of the time. It's great being the baby of the family because I always get my way, especially with Mom. She is a great cook. I wish I was as pretty as Mom."

"Well, Mrs. Huffman, the bell is going to ring in ten minutes, and I'm all done. I think your bulletin boards look a lot better. Can I ask you a question?"

"The bulletin boards have never looked this nice, Amy. Great job! What's your question?"

"What is your husband like? When you're with him at the ball games, you always look so happy. Does he spoil you?"

"Young lady, you are very perceptive. I am happy when we're together. He's a gentleman and does spoil me. He makes me feel like I'm the most important person in the world."

"That's the kind of guy I want to marry. I want him to spoil me and like the same things I like. He's got to be cute and taller than me. He's got to be nice because I want to have kids. I would only marry a guy who would be a good Dad. Don't you think that's important?"

"I can't think of anything more important, Amy. I have a feeling you'll meet a very nice guy. You deserve to have someone who will make you feel special."

The bell rang and Amy took her time getting her books together. I knew what was coming next.

"I know I can't get in trouble in study hall before the end of the semester, but if you ever need help with anything else, you could get me out of study hall. I'd be glad to help you. I'm a hard worker, you know, because I'm a Core."

"Amy Core, you will be the first person I ask for help. Let's shake on it."

I've just found my official helper for the year. Amy doesn't realize it, but I will be getting her out of study hall as often as possible.

Missing Amy

Journal Entry

October 1981

Amy has been out of school all week. There is a noticeable emptiness in the room without her. She's in the Toledo Children's Hospital for what she calls a 'clean out' of her lungs. I'm not surprised she's been hospitalized. She's coughed so much the past two weeks.

Most of the kids thought I was playing a joke on them today when they walked in the room and saw only two vocabulary words on the board. They know each Monday means fifteen new vocabulary words and a test on Friday.

The two vocabulary words are 'sympathy' and 'empathy.' I defined each word and put several examples on the board. Amy's name was never mentioned when I gave them examples of people for whom I've had sympathy and those for whom I've had empathy.

One of the boys sensed the words might be connected to Amy. He raised his hand and asked if she was still in the hospital because of her coughing. One of the girls was aggravated by his question and said, "She's got asthma. She can't help it."

I was cautious how I answered because it was apparent that many of them didn't know Amy had cystic fibrosis. If they had been told, they might not have understood at the time. I chose my words carefully.

"Amy's lungs aren't as strong and healthy as yours."

With two minutes remaining before class ended, I said, "If

19

you came back to school after being in the hospital several days, would you want sympathy or empathy from your classmates? Would you want them to feel sorry for you, or would you want them to try and understand what you were going through day after day when you coughed?"

"Raise your hands if Amy needs your sympathy."

They all looked around and no hands went up.

"Raise your hands if Amy needs your empathy."

No one looked around and everyone's hand went up.

After the bell rang, I said, "There is no vocabulary test on Friday. You all just passed with a perfect score. I'm proud of you."

Amy's Return

Journal Entry

October 1981

Amy came back to school today. I stood at the door and greeted her with a hug and a reminder of how much she'd been missed. She looked so tired and weak when she said, "It's good to be back."

We stayed after school together to go over homework assignments. There were two lists. One included assignments she needed to complete so I could be certain she understood the new material. The other list included additional writing assignments that I was not going to require her to do. I was trying to lighten her load, knowing she had a lot of homework in her other classes, too. She quickly saw through my plan and would have no part of it.

I casually said, "Amy, these are extra assignments. They're optional. You don't have to do them."

She raised her eyebrows with suspicion and said, "Did everybody else do them, Mrs. Huffman?"

"They did, Amy, but none of them have been sick and out of school several days."

Whit that, she reached over, picked up the optional list and said, "Then I'm going to do them, too."

At the end of each grading period, there were never any incomplete homework assignments beside Amy's name in my grade book.

On a day when she was feeling better, Amy wrote this poem in her journal. The assignment was to describe something you could see (but not touch) which left a lasting impression. Amy's poem symbolized her vibrant spirit.

21

Rainbows

Rainbows are colorful,

Rainbows are bright,

Rainbows make your day all right.

Rainbows cheer you up,

Rainbows never let you down,

When rainbows fade away

You walk back with a frown.

On a day when she wasn't feeling well, Amy wrote these telling words.

Dear God,

*Make my **UP's***

*Longer than my **DOWN'S!***

The Daily Struggles

The eighth graders worked all period on a writing assignment today. They were asked to describe their hero. Amy wasn't able to concentrate the minute class began. She tried so hard to muffle her coughs. As I looked over the shoulders of a few students to see what they were writing, I inched my way to her desk without drawing attention. I laid a cough drop in her lap and slid a note under her tablet encouraging her to get a drink of water.

As soon as she walked into the hall, the coughing erupted and took control of her body. Several drinks of water didn't help. I peered around the corner and saw her entering the restroom. After a few minutes passed, I asked the librarian to sit with my class while I checked on her.

The closer I got to the restroom, it sounded like she was choking. When I walked in, she was crying as drops of blood fell into the sink.

"Amy, are you coughing up blood?"

"No, my nose is bleeding because I coughed too hard. I'm okay, Mrs. Huffman. You can go back to class. I'm really okay."

She was quivering.

I hugged her and said, "Amy, I'm not going anywhere until this bleeding stops."

I dampened a paper towel from the dispenser and held it to her nose, while she willingly tilted her head back. Within a few minutes, the bleeding subsided. She kept repeating, "I'm sorry I got

23

blood on your sweater. I'm so sorry."

"It's no problem, Amy. I never liked this sweater anyhow."

She started to giggle, and we both laughed. As I wiped away her tears and a few remnants of dried blood, I said, "By the way, who is your hero? Who will be in your journal entry?"

"My mom," she said quietly.

"She's the perfect choice. Your mother is a wonderful lady. I've picked my hero, too, and it's someone you know. Take a guess."

She shrugged her shoulders and said, "I don't know."

"I'm picking you, Amy. You're my hero."

With eyes opened wide, she said, "You think I'm a hero? I can't wait to tell my sisters. They'll be so jealous."

As the bell rang, my hero headed to her next class.

Broken Wing

Journal Entry

November 1982

Amy stopped by my room early in the afternoon and asked if I would get her out of study hall today. I know she doesn't feel well by her pale color. She is coughing continually. The dramatic change in the cold, damp weather has affected how she feels.

After dropping off the permission slip to get her out of study hall, I stopped in the hallway to explain a homework assignment to a student. Consequently, I was a few minutes late returning to my room. When I walked in, Amy was in her seat. Her head was down and her eyes were closed. I picked up the pillow cushion that I had at the back of my chair.

"Amy, lay your head on this pillow. Do you want me to call your mother to come get you?"

"No, I can make it to the end of the day. I have a sinus headache. If I shut my eyes for a little bit, it will help."

I turned off the classroom lights.

"Just relax. If you fall asleep, I'll wake you up before your next class."

As I sat down to grade papers, she asked, "Mrs. Huffman, do you believe in God?"

There was silence. I walked over and sat down in the seat beside her.

"Amy, I believe in God with all my heart."

With her eyes still closed, she said, "You know, some days I believe in God and some days I don't. I keep praying that He will take away my disease, but He doesn't. There are miracles in the

25

Bible where He heals people, but He doesn't heal me. Did you know there is no cure for my cystic fibrosis?"

"I know there isn't. I'm so sorry. I pray for you every night."

She lifted her head and opened her eyes.

"Really? You pray for me? What do you say?"

"I thank God for giving you the strength to battle your disease like you do. Then I ask Him to continue giving you the strength you need to breathe easier."

"When did you start praying for me?"

"I prayed for you the first day of school last year. I asked God to help you through the many tough days ahead. I've never stopped praying for you."

"Could you write down the prayer you say, Mrs. Huffman? I think I'll start asking God for the same thing."

The bell rang.

As Amy reluctantly collected her books, she said, "Please keep praying for me. I need all the help I can get. See you tomorrow, Mrs. Huffman."

Dear Lord,

You must be so proud of Amy. She embraces each day with courage and conviction. She refuses to relinquish control to this unforgiving disease that has invaded her lungs and body forever. Somehow, she chooses to live life with freedom.

Amy asks for so little. She has prayed that You will make her UP'S longer than her DOWN'S. She simply wants to feel normal. She wants to breathe deeply and feel the air energize her body. She wants to escape from the shackles of her impaired lungs that will one day force her to say, "I surrender."

She dreams of falling in love with someone who will share her joy for the simple things in life that matter most. She wants to find a soul mate who will appreciate a note written in crayon that reads: "I love you."

She yearns to be a mother one day. She wants to be there when her child takes that first step and when the candles are blown out on the birthday cakes. She wants to see her child graduate from high school and enjoy a career. She wants to live long enough to hold her grandchildren.

I pray that her dreams are realized, Lord. Amy is like a fragile bird with one broken wing. She refuses to stop flying. Instead, she soars with one wing. Many days, she makes her flight appear effortless and free. Many days, she barely has the strength to lift her wing off the ground.

Thank you for watching over her. Only You know how many flights this fragile bird can make. Only You know how many breaths of air she will ultimately take.

Lord, thank you for Amy.

Amy Takes Charge

Journal Entry

December 1982

Amy was right when she told me she's a hard worker. I wrote a pass for her and a few of her friends to get out of study hall yesterday. They collated a lengthy handout for my high school seniors. Amy definitely likes taking charge. It was hard not to laugh when she began firing directives as to how she wanted things done. Her friends giggled and one of them said, "Yes, Mighty Leader! Your wishes are our commands."

I did a poor job of pretending not to listen, especially when Amy and her friend, Jayme were laughing to the point of tears. They recounted one of many eventful slumber parties in Amy's basement. They were proud of the night they stayed awake for hours and waited for their plan to unfold. When the others fell asleep, they put their friends' bras in the freezer. Although Amy was the instigator, she gave full credit to her sister, Cathy for giving her the idea. She proudly alerted her friends that she had many more tricks up her sleeve for future slumber parties.

The next topic of laughter involved the girls sarcastically reminding Amy of her blunder in a junior high girls' basketball game. According to Karen, everyone started shouting, "GO HORNETS!" when Amy got the ball. As Amy was running as fast as she could, everyone yelled, "YOU'RE GOING THE WRONG WAY, AMY!" Amy made the basket. Unfortunately, it was for the other team.

Once Amy started laughing hard, the inevitable followed. She started coughing. One of the girls grabbed a tissue from my

28

desk and handed it to her. Amy walked away from her assembly line of workers and said, "I need a drink, Mrs. Huffman. I'll be right back."

As soon as she left the room, one of her friends said, "She's okay. She coughs whenever she laughs too hard."

I smiled and said, "I love how all of you look out for her."

I would have complimented them more, but Amy returned. I looked at the girls and said, "You better get to work. Your boss is coming back."

The girls finished the job with five minutes showing on the clock. It was just enough time to reward their labors with Hershey kisses. As they gathered around my desk, one of them asked, "Mrs. Huffman, when did you start wearing nail polish?"

"Truthfully, it was in junior high. My English teacher wore nail polish, and I idolized her. Girls, it was a silly thing to do because the polish stains your nails."

Amy laid her hand on my desk and said, "I wish my fingernails looked like yours. Did you ever notice how weird my nails look because of my disease?"

There was an awkward silence when I put my hand on top of hers.

"Amy, I don't think your fingernails look weird. Mine look weird. They're painted with red nail polish that looks ridiculous with my pink sweater. Wouldn't you agree?"

Amy grinned.

"To tell you the truth, Mrs. Huffman, the colors do clash a little."

The bell rang, the girls dropped their candy wrappers in the wastebasket, and I reminded them how much I appreciated their help.

With dramatic authority, Amy said, "I'll probably hire you guys again for the next big job."

As soon as I got home from school, I removed my nail polish. I'm not going to wear any for the remainder of the school year.

Amy noticed my nails when she walked into the room today. She came up to the desk and quietly said, "Mrs. Huffman, you didn't have to take off your nail polish because you feel sorry for me."

I quietly whispered back, "I didn't do it because I feel sorry for you, Amy. I did it because I admire you."

Dear Amy

This is a difficult journal entry to write. I haven't yet told the administration that I have accepted a teaching position in my hometown next fall. Although it has been an emotional decision to make, it is the right decision to make for my family. Our son will soon be two years old, and I want to be in the same school system when he starts kindergarten.

It will be hard to say goodbye to my teaching colleagues and close friends. It will be even harder to say goodbye to my students, especially those in junior high. They think I will be returning next year to be their freshman English teacher.

I don't have the courage to say goodbye to Amy. She is counting on me to be her drama teacher. For now, I've decided to write her a letter.

Dear Amy,

How is it possible that your junior high years are nearly over, and next fall you will be in high school? I'm going to miss you more than you know. I'll never have another 'bulletin board girl' as dedicated as you...or as memorable.

You don't realize it, but you have taught me far more than I have taught you. I've learned so much by watching the way you handle adversity. You've taught me how essential it is to embrace the good days and endure the tough ones.

30

You don't know this, but I saw you for the first time when you were in second grade. It was a morning in May, and you were running in a race at recess. I can't remember whom you were competing against, but I do remember feeling sorry for your competitor because everyone was cheering for you. Now I know why. They were cheering for you on a warm, humid day when it was more difficult for you to breathe. You could have easily said, "I don't want to race today." You didn't. Instead, you competed when you knew the odds were against you.

Amy, that is why you are my hero. You awaken each morning and wonder if it will be easy to breathe...or difficult. Either way, you keep going. You've come to school many days when you didn't feel well. You could have said, "I don't feel like going to school today." You didn't. You came to school and disguised how you were physically feeling. You could have felt sorry for yourself and voiced this to people. You didn't In watching how you persevered, I have learned the true definition of courage.

Do you remember the journal topic I assigned when everyone was asked to describe the biggest wish they had for someone? I wrote about you. I know how much you dream of falling in love with a wonderful guy, getting married and being a mother. My wish is for these dreams to come true in your future.

Let me end with a quote by Helen Keller who said, "The most beautiful things cannot be seen or even touched...they must be felt with the heart." I think you are destined to teach many people the true meaning of these words, Amy, by the way you live your life. You will touch many hearts.

It has been such a privilege to have you in class. You have been my Annie Sullivan. You have been my teacher, Amy Jo Core.

With thanks and admiration,
Mrs. Huffman

P.S. Please don't get in trouble in study hall next year for talking too much!

31

Kindred Spirits

Amy is back in Toledo Children's Hospital. She's undergone a surgery to remove polyps from her nasal passages, another painful consequence of her disease. Despite her pleading with the doctor to let her go home early, he won't discharge this determined fourteen-year-old teenager until she's healed and feeling stronger.

When Lisa and her parents arrived at the hospital to see Amy, they were encouraged to hear they had the doctor's permission to take her out to eat. Normally, she would have grabbed the chance to break free from the confining hospital walls. This time was different. Despite much persuasion from her family, she didn't want to leave the room. Conspicuous white surgical tape covered her nose. Even though she was gaining strength daily, Amy wasn't emotionally prepared to shield the painful stares from people at the restaurant.

Lisa was determined to lift her sister's spirits. Upon spotting a roll of white surgical tape lying on Amy's night stand, Lisa cut two strips and covered her own nose. As Amy, Bob and Leona continued laughing, Lisa reached for Amy's hand, helped her off the bed and said, "Come on, Amos. We're getting out of here. Let's go eat pizza."

When they arrived at the restaurant, Amy ate as much pepperoni pizza as she possibly could and ignored the obvious onlookers. Lisa didn't want to ruin the evening so she pretended not to notice the rude people who were fixated on the two sisters' facial appearances. She wasn't going to let anyone or anything rob her sister of this good time.

Amy wanted to delay her return to the hospital as long as possible. So did her family. The days in the hospital seemed endless. The television shows were continual repeats, there were constant interruptions from the nurses and doctors and there was never the opportunity to get a full night's rest. All of this weighed on Amy. It weighed on her family, too. Their hearts ached in accepting the brutal truth that Amy's life would be dictated by many unbearable days, weeks and months spent in hospitals.

Amy did, however, experience the blessing of friendship during this hospital stay. She bonded immediately with her fifteen-year-old roommate, Barb, who was born with a bowel obstruction; further testing at birth indicated she had cystic fibrosis. While Amy suffered primarily with pulmonary problems, Barb suffered with intestinal maladies and diabetes. Eventually, the same types of pulmonary issues that Amy endured as a teenager would take control of Barb's life as a young adult.

Neither of the girls previously had a close friend who battled the same debilitating disease. Their friendship, however, was based on far more than this. Amy and Barb soon discovered they were equally spunky, strong-willed and competitive, especially when they had wheelchair races in the hallway. They delighted in annoying one of the older nurses when they slipped out of their room, jumped in their wheelchairs and sped away. Finally, the girls' daring natures proved to be too stressful and the nurse reported their antics to their doctor.

Unfortunately, the doctor's reaction was not what the nurse expected. He explained that the girls were bored and weren't hurting anything. In fact, he thought the wheelchair races provided good exercise for their lungs.

When Amy and Barb weren't giggling about cute boys, they were voicing total disapproval of the hospital food and their dread of daily breathing treatments. They felt one another's emotional pain when they coughed in public, and people looked at them as if they were contagious. Most of all, Amy and Barb shared the same passionate will to live. Based on frightening medical statistics at the time, the girls were certain they could beat the odds and live longer than the doctors expected.

Amy and Barb shared the same hopes and dreams. They wanted to one day marry caring men and have children. Neither one of them forgot the day their doctor tried to spoil these dreams when he said they should never get pregnant. They heard him firmly say, "Having children could put your lives in jeopardy."

The doctor emphasized that a pregnancy would be too stressful on the girls' lungs, and raising young children would be too physically demanding on their bodies. As soon as the doctor finished

33

talking and left the room, the two friends looked at each other as if to say, "He didn't change our minds one bit about having children."

Even though cystic fibrosis pillaged the girls' bodies, it never weakened their spirits. Amy and Barb formed a kindred friendship that was meant to last a lifetime...and it did.

The Bet

Amy's senior year was spent having fun with her friends. She continued to get as much physical exercise as possible and especially looked forward to being on the volleyball team. Although she wasn't a starting player, she hustled to her position and played to win.

The volleyball team had won the conference title the previous year. Chris, the volleyball coach, had t-shirts made that reflected the previous winning season. The team ran a serve-receive formation called a 'stack.' The t-shirts were designed with the 'stack formation' on the back with the caption: 'We're stacked in '86.' It was meant to be a play on words. The team played 'the stack formation' and had many good players.

When Amy saw the shirts, she loudly proclaimed, "Finally, I get to be stacked!" Everyone on the team howled with laughter.

As much as Amy enjoyed playing volleyball, she enjoyed flirting even more with a cute boy in the junior class. Between classes, Amy found herself staring at Terry Greer. Between classes, Terry found himself staring at Amy Core. Although Amy didn't know him, Karen did from having ridden the same school bus for years. As fate would have it, Terry sat at the study hall table behind Amy and Karen. Although Karen might not have realized it at first, she quickly discovered that she would be taking on the role of matchmaker for Terry and her best friend.

Terry was on the wrestling team his junior year and paid close attention to Amy, one of the statisticians. He debated when to make his move and ask her for a date. One day during wrestling practice, Terry asked Amy's cousin, Jay, if he thought Amy would date him. Jay's quick response was, "There's NO WAY she'd go out with you!"

Terry smiled with confidence and said, "You wanna bet on that?"

Seizing the opportunity in study hall the next day, Terry passed a note to Karen. He asked what she thought his chances were of Amy going out with him. With Terry's note in hand, Karen leaned over and whispered, "Amy, will you go out with Terry if he asks?"

Amy's grin said it all.

Terry won the bet with Jay. He also won Amy's heart forever.

Certainty

Upon graduating from high school in 1987, Amy enrolled for fall classes at the University of Northwestern Ohio in Lima, Ohio, to pursue an associate's degree in business administration. Terry thought it was in Amy's best interest if they stopped dating before she started college.

Knowing he still had to finish his senior year of high school, Terry didn't want to hold Amy back from dating other guys, especially since he planned to enlist in the service after graduation. He didn't want her to feel tied down to him.

Amy was against breaking up and was miserable the two months they were apart. Terry was miserable, too. This breaking-up period solidified their feelings for one another even more.

Their mutual friends, Heather and Greg, brought them together again. They knew Terry was going to be at his friend's house one night and they just happened to stop by with Amy. Terry didn't know about the plan, but Amy did. Once they reunited, they never broke up again.

Following his high school graduation in 1988, Terry enlisted in the Air Force and was sent to boot camp in San Antonio, Texas for eight weeks. Being away from Amy those eight weeks felt like eight years. The best part of his day was when the mail arrived. He knew there would be a care package of food or a letter from her every day. The packages were only allowed to be a certain size, and Terry got in trouble the day she sent far too much food. He and his buddies, however, enjoyed every extra cookie Amy had baked.

They wrote lengthy letters to each other. Amy updated him on her college classes and continually shared how proud she was of him. At the top of each letter, she wrote 'I LOVE YOU!' in bold red or green ink. She signed every letter or card with 'I love you, babe. Always and Yours Forever, Amy.'

Terry called whenever the soldiers were given permission

to contact their loved ones. Since the breaks were only 30 minutes long, there was always a line of soldiers waiting to use the pay phone. Terry stood in the rain for 30 minutes one day waiting to call Amy, but by the time he got to the phone, the break was over. She never left the house that weekend waiting for his call. Amy was his lifeline, and he felt terrible that he had disappointed her.

Although she had never flown before, nothing was going to stop Amy from being at Terry's graduation ceremony from boot camp. On February 16, 1989, she flew from the airport in Toledo, Ohio to the Dallas/Fort Worth airport. From there, she took a commercial bus to San Antonio. Terry's sister, Anna, and his brother-in-law didn't live far from the base, so Terry made arrangements for them to meet Amy at the bus terminal and bring her to graduation.

When the officers dismissed the soldiers from their formation at the end of the graduation ceremony, they all ran to find their families. Terry scoured the crowd for Amy and spotted her before she saw him. Once he held her in his arms, he couldn't let go. They yearned to be husband and wife and began making plans to be married October 21, 1989 in Amy's home church, the Powell Memorial United Methodist Church.

Weeks before the wedding, Bob had a long talk with his brother, Tom. Due to Amy's serious health problems, he and Leona worried about her getting married. Tom told Bob that with everything Amy had been through, she was tougher than all the Cores put together. Tom also said it would take a very strong, dedicated man to take care of her, and Terry seemed like the man who could do it. Bob and Leona felt the same way.

Based on medical statistics at the time they were married, Amy had a chance to live another four or five years. Terry ignored the statistics. He was determined to be with Amy for the rest of her life.

Starting Over

There were several moves and many adjustments ahead for the newlyweds. After they were married, Amy moved to Michigan as soon as Terry found an apartment off base. After being together only three months, he was shipped to Panama. When he returned home three months later, they felt like they were starting over.

During those months in Michigan, Amy worked at a group home with people who had various disabilities. She enjoyed working with these teenagers and adults and made a conscious effort to compliment them and make them feel important. She empathized in knowing how frustrating it was to be denied the opportunity to live a normal life.

Amy stayed in close touch with her family and friends and was thrilled when anyone came to visit. Lisa and her husband, Brad took Bob and Leona to see Amy and Terry one weekend to watch an air show at the base. This was a fond memory for everyone. In spite of their limited finances, Amy and Terry made a deliberate effort to make sure everyone had a good time. Although they lived in a small, two-bedroom apartment, they made their families and friends feel comfortable. Somehow, they always found a way to make the best of things.

For their first wedding anniversary, Amy gave Terry specific orders not to spend a lot of money. Instead, she wanted him to make her something and she promised to do the same for him. The day of their anniversary, he walked into the apartment and was greeted by the warm smell of chocolate chip cookies. By no means were they ordinary chocolate chip cookies. Amy had shaped the cookie dough to spell the words: I Love You!

Terry had an equally sentimental gift for his sweetheart. He found a woodshop business off base. After Terry explained to the owner what he wanted made, the artisan did a beautiful job of applying Terry and Amy's wedding picture to a piece of wood that he custom designed in the shape of a heart. The anniversary surprise didn't end there. Terry wrote a poem that the artisan engraved beside their wedding picture. This loving and caring symbol hung above their bed the rest of their married life.

Amy Means Love

How I found you I'll never know,

It must have been God's love that really showed.

Without your love I could not live

And all the care that you give.

And with all that I feel I belong,

If we're together what could be wrong.

Your hugs and kisses are so sweet

And the way we met was pretty neat.

How lucky I am to be loved by you,

Only my best I'll try to do.

If we're strong and our love does grow,

We'll be the only two who really know

What Love means!

I Love You!

October 21, 1989

Being together changed dramatically when Terry received orders to go to Turkey for a year during the first Gulf War. At that point, they decided it was best if Amy moved back with her parents. Once his final tour of duty was finished, Terry was relieved that he would never be separated from Amy again. They made the decision to return home and rent a house trailer near Mt. Cory.

For a year, Terry farmed with Bob before being hired as a yard supervisor at a local lumberyard. While working there, Amy came to Terry's job site one day with the exciting news she was pregnant. Amy's immediate joy became immediate concern for Terry and Amy's family. Her physician had strongly advised against a pregnancy because of the stress and risks it could impose on her brittle health. Amy, however, wanted to be a mother and chose to ignore her doctor's warnings.

Amy's sisters weren't surprised when she got pregnant because Amy usually did what she set out to do. In their eyes, God blessed Amy and Terry with the pregnancy. By God's grace, this baby would give Amy the ultimate will to live in the years ahead.

Amy's Miracle

Leona was extremely concerned. She was haunted by the doctor's warnings ten years earlier when he explained the potentially dire consequences of a pregnancy.

Leona shared these fears more than once with her sister, Helen. Mothers always worry about their children, but Leona carried an even greater burden because of Amy's health. When she and Bob learned Amy had cystic fibrosis, Helen realized that Leona's life would never be the same. She would be afraid each day of Amy's life. Although she did her best to conceal her fears, Leona was terrified for Amy and the baby she was carrying.

During the pregnancy, Amy developed gestational diabetes, which the doctors were able to monitor. Beyond that, the pregnancy went well, much to everyone's surprise and relief. On July 28, 1993, Amy gave birth to a healthy 6 lb. 12 oz. baby girl. The newborn was immediately tested for cystic fibrosis and the results were negative.

Throughout the pregnancy, Amy and Terry thought they'd have a boy and decided early on that his name would be Eric. They hadn't considered a girl's name. When their daughter was born, they named her Erica. They were certain they wanted their child's middle name to be 'Lee' after Terry's younger brother, Darren Lee Greer. While Amy was pregnant, Darren, who was twenty years old at the time, lost control of his vehicle on a patch of ice and slid broadside into the path of a van. He and his friend were killed. Amy and Terry always regretted that Darren never had the chance to know their daughter, Erica Lee Greer.

From the moment she was born, Amy called Erica her "miracle baby." Erica truly was a medical miracle in many respects. When Amy was initially diagnosed with CF, half of the people who had the disease did not live past their early twenties. Most women with CF who lived into adulthood had great difficulty becoming pregnant and carrying their babies to full term.

When Amy's friends, Karen and Julie, went to the hospital to meet the newest addition to the Greer family, they were so moved by Amy's joy. This new mother felt like she had been given a precious gift from God.

After three days in the hospital, Terry was able to bring his family home. Amy's body and spirit seemed miraculously strengthened. Her maternal love was captured in Erica's baby book.

First Thoughts about Baby:

Erica was so tiny, and as soon as I held her, she was so quiet and content. She is the most beautiful miracle I have ever seen. I loved her the second she was born.

Wishes and Messages for Baby:

I wish for my baby girl to have a long, happy and healthy life. I wish for my daughter to pursue her dreams and not hold back for anything. She must follow her dream and accomplish it, no matter what. I wish for my daughter to find a love of her life who will make her happy and share everything with her.

Erica, I love you.

Mom

God's Plan

Amy was doing well as she continued her daily breathing treatments, made her yearly 'clean out' trips to the hospital, and took good care of herself. She was healthy enough to work full time as an account representative for the Hancock County Human Services Division in Findlay. Terry enjoyed working on the surveying crew for Van Horn, Hoover and Associates in Findlay. They were excited about purchasing their first home in the country outside Rawson.

In 1992, Amy had the physical stamina to play in an adult volleyball league and impressed her new teammates the first time they met. One such teammate, Larry, was struck by the energy that Amy brought to the game. He knew she had CF, but it wasn't apparent when her slender body would jump high, slide low and dig for the loose ball with tenacity. Amy never showed signs of fatigue. Despite coughing a few times each set, she never labored for air.

Amy's teammates found her especially entertaining when she made it profoundly clear to the referees that she disagreed with some of their calls. As Amy battled her opponents, no one could have known the personal health battle that was playing out inside her body.

Without warning, Amy's world changed when she got pneumonia in 1997. She and Terry received the traumatic news from the doctors that her lung capacity had deteriorated dramatically over the past years. Cystic fibrosis had wreaked permanent damage to her lungs, and she was advised to get on a transplant list as soon as possible.

Amy and Terry were stunned. They weren't prepared to hear this despairing news, let alone believe it. They traveled to the University of Pittsburgh Hospital and the Cleveland Clinic for second and third opinions. The medical diagnosis was the same. Amy needed new lungs in order to live. It was an eighteen-month wait for a double lung transplant at each medical facility. By this point, Amy found it

44

incredibly tiring to work four or five hours a day. Ultimately, she didn't have the physical strength to continue working. Her application for permanent disability benefits was approved July 24, 1997.

Knowing they would be facing major health bills, Amy and Terry put their home on the market and rented a farmhouse. While living there, Amy received a phone call in late 1997 from Loyola University Hospital in Chicago. She was told their waiting list for transplant patients was fourteen to sixteen months. Due to the shorter wait time, she decided to go on the transplant list at Loyola. At that point, she and Terry carried beepers, hoping they would get the call that she was a compatible match with an organ donor.

The evening of April 6, 1998, Deb and Lisa met Amy at the Blanchard Valley Hospital in Findlay to hear a young man talk about his lung transplant experience. Amy asked him questions with curiosity and confidence. Once she heard what the young man had gone through and survived, she believed she could do the same. Her family believed it, too. They had witnessed Amy survive other grave moments when the doctors gave her little hope. By now, she was on oxygen during the day and grew winded after climbing two or three steps. Time had become her enemy. What follows are the thoughts, fears and prayers Lisa wrote in her journal that evening.

Amy was late and so was the presenter. She wore a red outfit and looked very nice. I was actually going to tell her and never had the opportunity or took the time.

The young man talked about his transplant and Amy asked questions. I believe it was comforting for her to know he had made it through and was doing well. Afterwards, we went for a burger and malt. Amy didn't have any money so I covered her meal. We chatted awhile and talked about things to come. Small talk. Nothing serious. We're always too busy to take the time to talk seriously about anything.

Why do we face health problems like this? Why don't we live in a perfect world? There is a greater, divine power watching over us. We must depend on Him.

"I can do all things through Christ who strengthens me."
Philippians 4:13

Dear God, please bless Amy. Give her the strength she needs to survive. Help her beat this. Give her a guardian angel. Please.

Amy and her family didn't realize that God already had a plan in motion.

Sisters Helping Sisters

The original plan on April 6th had been for Bob, Leona and Jill to also attend the young man's transplant presentation at the hospital. Earlier that day, however Jill faced a tragedy no one saw coming.

Shortly after lunch, an office aide came to Jill's elementary classroom and said her husband was on the phone. Something had to be terribly wrong because Mike had never called her during the school day. When Jill answered, he was crying and told her to get to the hospital immediately because his dad had suffered a heart attack.

Jill quickly left instructions for the rest of her classes. Every second of her 30-minute drive from Ottawa to Findlay was spent crying, praying and making bargains with God to spare the life of her father-in-law, Merrill. Shortly after she arrived at the hospital, the doctors said there was nothing they could do. Merrill had passed away. Later, Mike and Jill would need to explain to their three young daughters why Grandpa wouldn't be coming home ever again.

Three days earlier, the emotional scenario had been significantly different for Bob, Leona and their daughters. On Friday morning, April 3rd, Deb had received the wonderful news from her social worker that her plans to adopt two young sisters, ages six and three, were finalized. Deb quickly began preparations to travel overseas to see her daughters, Maria and Aly, for the first time. The excitement in knowing she would soon be a Mom was overwhelming.

When Deb had begun the necessary paperwork to adopt several months earlier, Leona had planned to travel with her. This changed when Amy's name went on the transplant list. Leona would be traveling to Chicago with Amy and Terry when new lungs were available. Deb's good friend, Jan, readily offered to take Leona's

47

place. While Deb was filled with joy in knowing she would soon be hugging her daughters, she was extremely concerned for Amy who was failing day by day. Everyone in the family was afraid to voice the fear that Amy wouldn't receive a lung transplant in time. Based on the medical literature they read, it seemed like the waiting period to receive a lung transplant took forever.

'Forever' was about to change. Amy called her sisters shortly after 2 a.m. on April 7th with miraculous news. She was on her way to receive a new pair of lungs. When the phone rang so early, Deb was afraid to answer in fear of bad news. Instead, it was Amy whose voice was filled with hope.

When Amy called Lisa, they said, "I love you" to each other. After they hung up, Lisa was overcome with sadness and worry. Everyone knew this transplant was a huge risk. Everyone knew Amy could die.

In Jill's mind, her father-in-law was Amy's guardian angel. Sleep was no longer an option for the sisters. Their hearts were one as they prayed for Amy.

The Lung Transplant

When Amy's name was placed on the lung transplant list, she and Terry took transplant preparation classes at Loyola University Medical Center in Chicago. The trainer walked them through the steps like a dress rehearsal. One of the first things he told them to do was pack their bags as soon as they returned home. He was also very frank in explaining what Amy's surgery would involve and the necessary care required afterwards.

Amy was warned that she could get to the hospital and be told the lungs were not a compatible match. Some people get three or four calls and find it's a 'no go' at the last minute. The lungs must match in size, and the donor must have the same blood type. As the trainer explained that the lungs were only viable so many hours, he emphasized how crucial it was to get to the hospital immediately. Amy and Terry were told everything that could go right with the transplant as well as everything that could go wrong. They were reminded several times that it would feel like 'a do or die moment' when the call came.

When Amy received her call, the voice at the other end said, "We have a set of lungs. Get on a plane and get to Loyola immediately!"

Anxiety raced through Amy and Terry's veins. They were shocked to receive the call after being on the transplant list only three months. They tried to stay grounded emotionally. Terry called Bob and Leona immediately, while Amy tried to gently awaken Erica.

Within minutes, Bob and Leona arrived. Bob and Amy argued all the way to the Bluffton airport about Erica. Bob said she wasn't getting on the plane, and Amy said she was. Bob said he and Amy's sisters would look after her until the surgery was over, and Amy said Erica was coming with them. Amy won the argument.

49

The pilot was waiting for them when they arrived. The Loyola transplant team had contacted him at the same time they called Amy. The minute the family boarded, the plane took off. Even though Erica was only four years old and confused by everything, she remembered wearing her pajamas on the airplane, holding her stuffed animal, Kitty, and receiving a blanket from the pilot because she was cold.

Before the family knew it, the plane began to descend. As they peered out the windows, the sun was rising in Chicago. The horizon cast a warm glow and God's presence could be felt.

The instant the plane landed, there was an ambulance waiting for Amy. She had seconds to hug her family goodbye before the transplant team loaded her on a gurney and raced to the hospital. Another car quickly transported Erica, Leona and Terry. Once Amy was prepped for surgery, the family saw her a few seconds before she was wheeled to the operating room.

Terry and Leona stayed in a surgery waiting room. As it turned out, Amy made the right decision for Erica to come. She was a good distraction for Terry and Leona, as she frequently asked for food and drinks from the vending machines and played in the children's area.

During the first four hours of surgery, Terry and Leona didn't eat or drink anything while they waited for someone to say how the surgery was going. A short time later, two chaplains walked into the waiting room and said, "Are Terry and Leona here?"

Leona broke down and cried. Terry went numb with fear. They thought the chaplains had come to tell them Amy had died. Instead, the men had come to comfort them with a prayer. The chaplains reached out with their hearts and hands and everyone prayed together for Amy.

Finally, one of the surgeons spoke with them after a surgery that took over seven hours. Although he explained the surgery had gone as well as possible, he cautiously said, "Time will tell. We'll wait and see."

Amy was immediately put on anti-rejection drugs and was taken to the intensive care unit. When Terry and Leona were given permission to see her, they weren't emotionally prepared. Her frail body was connected to multiple machines, and there were different breathing tubes going into her mouth. Erica was scared and started to cry. Even though Amy couldn't talk, she mouthed the words, "I love you" to Erica. Terry and Leona wept in relief.

Within a few minutes, Erica stopped crying and climbed into

Amy's bed. More tears flowed when Erica reached over the tubes and hugged her mom. The next several days were going to be critical. Amy's survival depended on her body's ability to accept the new lungs.

After the Transplant

Lisa and Bob traveled to Chicago to see Amy the day after her surgery. When they arrived at the hospital, Leona was there to meet them. Her weary eyes revealed the deluge of stress and worry from the past few days. Although Amy was doing well, there were multiple fears running through everyone's mind.

Before Bob and Lisa were allowed to see Amy, they had to wash their hands and put on gowns and masks. It was overwhelming to see her connected to all the breathing tubes and numerous machines. As Lisa held her sister's hand, Amy tried to communicate by using her fingers to spell out the letters i-c-e.c...in the palm of Lisa's hand. Amy wanted ice chips, but the nurse said she couldn't have any because of the tubes going down her throat. Lisa struggled to hold back tears. Crying was the last thing she wanted to do in front of her brave sister.

After Bob and Lisa visited with Amy, Lisa followed Terry down the hall. Sensing he was upset, she caught up with him in the stairwell and asked if he was all right. With tears of fatigue in his eyes, he said, "I'm fine." Lisa realized the flight, the lack of sleep and the intense wait for Amy to come out of surgery had taken a tremendous toll on him.

Five days after the surgery, Bob, Jill and Deb visited Amy. When they reached her room, they were told to stand in the hall because the doctors were examining her. The two sisters just looked at each other with facial expressions that said, "Can't they hurry? Don't they know we're out here?" The sisters laughed nervously. They had to see with their own eyes that Amy was okay.

In her sisters' eyes, Amy looked wonderful. Amy asked Deb, the hairdresser in the family to shampoo her hair right away. Even though it was a challenge, Deb and Jill managed. They found themselves thinking that only Amy would have the stamina to have her hair washed just five days after receiving new lungs.

Amy was excited to hear about Deb's adoption plans and

listened carefully as Deb explained that she would be leaving Thursday. While Deb was outwardly sharing her excitement about the upcoming trip, she was inwardly concealing her concern for Amy.

After being in the hospital only nine days, Amy was doing so well that the doctors allowed her to move into a fully furnished apartment that Terry found near the hospital. A benevolent couple paid their apartment rent for the first two months. This couple chose to remain anonymous. In their humble words, they wanted "to give all the glory to God."

Later in May, Jill was able to return to Chicago and spend a week with Amy and Erica. They spent time watching television, playing games, talking and laughing. Jill continually found herself thinking, "I'm so grateful to be here with my sister."

Family, friends, church congregations, co-workers, neighbors and entire communities had been praying for Amy's lung transplant to go well. Their prayers were answered. Amy's body continued to accept her new lungs.

The Apartment

A double lung transplant does not cure someone who has cystic fibrosis because it never goes away, even though the transplanted lungs come from donors who do not have the disease. The recipient still has CF in the sinuses, pancreas, intestines, sweat glands and reproductive tract.

Before Amy's transplant, she took approximately 25 pills each day to help with digestion and lung issues. After the transplant, she took more than 70 pills daily that included lung anti-rejection medications and drugs to fight infection. To stop the immune system from rejecting the new lungs, the immunosuppressive drugs have to be taken for life. These drugs may cause side effects that include diabetes, kidney problems, cancer-like tumors and osteoporosis. The drugs may also decrease the body's ability to fight germs like 'pseudomonas aeruginosa' that may stay in the upper airways after a transplant and infect the lungs.

Terry and Leona spent the first few weeks in the apartment making sure everything was set up correctly with Amy's medications. They were also trained to monitor the drainage tubes and to assist her with specific exercises. Although Amy wasn't on oxygen when she left the hospital, she was connected to a device that electronically recorded her vitals. Each day, she dialed a phone number that transmitted information directly to the hospital. This way, the doctors and nurses could adjust her medications accordingly. Nurses, physical therapists and dietitians came to the apartment regularly to help her gain more strength in the recovery process.

Amy and Terry couldn't have gotten through everything without Leona. Her presence was crucial. She helped take care of Amy and Erica, prepared the meals and kept the apartment extremely clean and free of any germs. Beyond that, Amy wanted her mother there. Throughout her life, she felt more secure knowing Leona was with her, especially during the gravely critical times. Even though the entire family encouraged Leona to take a break periodically and return home, she wouldn't go until she felt completely comfortable leaving Amy.

Eventually, a schedule was worked out. When one of Amy's sisters could stay with her through the week, Terry went home to work and then drove back to Chicago on weekends. This help from Amy's sisters enabled Leona to return home for short periods of time.

Amy liked getting outside as much as possible. There were a few restaurants near the apartment that were within walking distance for her. There were also a few stores where Amy and her sisters shopped. Each step outside the apartment provided Amy the opportunity to exercise and build her strength. Even though Erica was so young, she knew her mom was feeling much better. No one needed to tell her. Erica instinctively reached for her mother's hand whenever there was a chance to leave the apartment and do something as a family.

In April of 1998, Amy composed the following letter that she sent to the many people in her home church who provided emotional, spiritual and financial support during and after the transplant:

Dear Friends,

*God **does** answer prayers. He has answered all the prayers sent to Him on my behalf. For those prayers, I thank you. In case you've not heard, my lung transplant surgery went well. God sent His best angels as well as His best doctors and nurses to watch over me. They worked miracles. I was released from the hospital nine days after surgery!*

The journey is far from over. I am now living in an apartment ten minutes from my Chicago hospital, Loyola University. The doctors say I could be here approximately three months, but I'm praying for a speedier recovery.

My days consist of therapy, medicines, exercising, resting and more medicines and therapy. I've only had one major scare and that was when my left lung filled up with mucus and fluids, forcing me to spend a few days in the hospital while the doctors cleaned me out and ran a biopsy on some lung tissue. The test results were good, and there is no rejection so far!

My success has many contributing factors. God, first and foremost has given me a new chance to live for Him. Secondly, my family has been with me throughout the entire ordeal. In fact, my four-year-old daughter, Erica, has been with me in Chicago since the transplant.

My husband, Terry, has been tirelessly wonderful and always lovingly by my side, handling the hundreds of tasks in Chicago as well as keeping "our home fires burning." Of course, my parents have been a godsend, just as all my sisters and their families have been.

The third, and certainly one of the most crucial factors in my miraculous recovery has been the prayer support of you friends who are my family in God's house. Without your support and prayers, I know in my heart that the outcome of this surgery would have been different.

Life will be different for me forever. I could sit back, look at the medical bills, the cost of the pills and the strain it has put on everyone, but God won't let me. I count my blessings daily and hope you do, too. I hope you've talked with your loved ones about organ donations that save lives. I'm living proof.

I hope that you will be able to attend the musical tribute being hosted by the Powell Memorial United Methodist Church on May 10th. I've heard many of these people sing and I'm telling you, they can "sing their lungs out"...no pun intended.

My greatest hope is to be home for the chicken barbecue on June 26th so I can be living, breathing proof of the miracles that God can work.

Keep me in your thoughts and prayers,
Amy Greer and Family.

After two months in the apartment, Terry planned a big surprise for his wife and daughter. He rented a limousine, bought Amy a new black dress and purse and purchased tickets to see *The Phantom of the Opera*. He wouldn't reveal his plans until Amy and Erica were all dressed up so he could take his two best girls out on the town.

The limo driver took the Greer family on a tour of downtown Chicago. They saw the Sears Tower and Michigan Avenue before the show. Terry had a bottle of champagne ready to share with Amy and a bottle of Mountain Dew for Erica. When he opened the limo's sunroof, Amy and Erica stood up and took in the view.

Amy kept asking, "Terry, how much did this cost?"

While Leona had been in Chicago taking care of Amy and

Erica, her mind was also on Deb who was finalizing the adoptions. This devoted Grandma was excited in knowing that she and Bob would soon go from having six granddaughters to eight.

When Deb and her daughters arrived home on April 25th after more than twenty hours of traveling, they were exhausted. Maria and Aly had bronchitis and Deb had a cold. When Leona came home from Chicago that weekend to meet her granddaughters, she had to be careful that she didn't catch anything because she was soon returning to Chicago to stay with Amy.

Even though Deb had sent Amy many pictures of her girls, she couldn't wait for Amy to meet them. Deb looked forward to Amy coming home. Then their family would feel whole again.

Coming Home

By the end of May, Amy was doing very well. Her doctors were willing to let her go home, if she followed the medical protocol they had established for her. She was required to return to Chicago every three months for a check-up. Additionally, she was required to be under the care of a pulmonary specialist who could treat her lung-related issues as well as the diabetes and pseudomonas virus she developed from the transplant.

As excited as Amy and Terry were to return home, they were extremely nervous. They had a safety net while they were in the apartment. If the slightest thing went wrong, Amy had immediate medical care. They were going from living in a medical environment to essentially living on their own. Before leaving Chicago, Amy's medical team contacted Dr. Watson at Blanchard Valley Hospital in Findlay. This was a huge relief to Amy and Terry. In the years ahead, he would remain her primary pulmonary specialist whom they trusted and respected.

On My 27th, Amy returned home. Bob and Leona were there to greet them. A 'Welcome Home' sign was hanging above the door and yellow ribbons swayed from the trees and basketball pole. Freshly planted flowers framed the house. The warm greeting didn't end there. Weeks earlier, Amy's sisters and Terry's brother, Brad had cleaned, decorated and painted several rooms in the house. It felt so good to be home. Amy couldn't stop smiling as they pulled into their driveway.

This marked the beginning of Amy's strenuous journey to recovery. Leona stayed with her during the days until Terry returned home from work. For several weeks, Leona and Amy's sisters prepared the family's meals. After being home six months, she had regained a great deal of strength. Even though she could breathe on her own, the weather was often a factor in how she felt.

When there was a lot of humidity in the air or a sudden change in the weather, it was more difficult to breathe or walk very far. When Amy had a good day, she made the most of it.

In addition to carefully monitoring her diabetes, Amy had to be extremely mindful of avoiding crowds or being near someone who was sick. A minor cold for most people could turn into a major lung infection for her. Although she had a few flare-ups with lung problems that required trips to the hospital, she got along well the first year after the transplant.

While Amy was on a personal mission to continue doing well, her sisters were on their own mission. They were involved with people from their church and the surrounding communities in organizing fund-raisers to help defray the costs of Amy's enormous medical expenses.

Breathing Easier

LeAnn Grose, a staff writer for the *Courier* in Findlay, Ohio interviewed Amy soon after she was home from Chicago. What follows are excerpts from the feature story that was published June 11, 1998 with the headline: 'Lung Transplant Recipient Breathing Easier.'

Amy (Core) Greer, 29, of Rawson is proof organ transplants can work. On April 7, Amy, who was diagnosed with cystic fibrosis at age 9, received a new set of lungs at Chicago's Loyola Hospital. Amy, as well as her family and friends have been breathing easier ever since.

"This whole ordeal has brought organ donation awareness to my family, my church and my community," Amy said. "I think people think about maybe becoming donors now because I'm proof that organ donation really works."

In September of 1998, Amy went for a regular 'clean out' at Toledo Hospital but didn't get her usual pep back and still could not breathe easily.

"After the treatment in September, I didn't feel rarin' to go like I usually do," Amy recalled.

Further tests and x-rays indicated that the disease had progressed to the point where cysts were growing in her lungs and the fibroid tissue was blocking many of her bronchial passages.

From October up until the transplant, Amy was on oxygen nearly all the time. She couldn't climb stairs or even walk across a room without growing short of breath.

After numerous treatments in Toledo and Cleveland, Amy went to Chicago in January for an evaluation and was immediately placed on the list for a transplant. The doctors told her it wouldn't take long to find a match since she had a B-positive blood type, the most common.

After receiving the transplant call, Amy commented, "I wasn't scared. The hospital really prepares you as to what is going to happen. But it sure is a weird feeling to have part of somebody else in you."

As Amy and her husband, Terry were quickly preparing for the flight to Chicago, Amy needed to explain to their four-year-old daughter what was happening. "I just tried to explain to Erica, 'Mom's going to go get new lungs." She didn't like it at first when she saw me in the hospital with all the tubes and wires but she adjusted fast," Amy said. "And my husband is the most wonderful guy-he's right there every time I go into the hospital."

After a seven-hour surgery, Amy spent nine days in the hospital before moving to a nearby apartment in Chicago where she lived until May 27th. The doctors there wanted her to be close to the hospital just in case her body rejected the new lungs. She also had to be there for regular check-ups. "But when I first got out of the hospital, I just didn't feel any different," she said. "I kept coughing and wheezing like before. But after I had a bronchoscopy, I felt 95 percent better.

A bronchoscopy involves placing a tube with an electric light and tiny "camera" down the inside of the windpipe and into the lungs to check the bronchial tubes that are cleared if necessary.

Amy still has CF but because the new lungs' cells are "programmed" differently, the CF won't be able to attack them. She will still have sinus drainage and the poor digestion caused by CF and has also developed diabetes because of all the medication. She can breathe on her own again and that's what matters.

The following article appeared in the *Courier* in conjunction with the interview:

Church Plans Barbecue

Amy Greer and her family are facing expenses of more than $250,000 including her lung transplant surgery, doctors' and surgeons' fees, the hospital stays, living expenses in Chicago, medication and follow-up care.

Amy's medical insurance will not cover all the bills. To help defray the expenses, Powell Memorial United Methodist Church, which Amy has attended with her family since childhood, is sponsoring a Harlan's Chicken Barbecue on June 26 from 4:30 to 7:30 p.m. at the Jenera Community Building.

61

Proceeds will go to the Powell Memorial Benevolent Fund for Amy Greer to which contributions may also be sent in care of the church at 9648 County Road 313, Findlay, Ohio, 45840.

The church is also promoting awareness and education about organ donation, requesting people sign donor cards and discuss the possibility of becoming donors. Donor cards are available at the Hancock County License Bureau.

In addition to this benefit, another one was held May 10, 1998, which was a musical tribute hosted by Amy's church. A free-will offering was given with the proceeds going to the benevolent fund that had been established for Amy.

In the years ahead, people from the area and surrounding communities continued to contribute to this fund with such devotion and generosity that Amy and her entire family were overwhelmed by the benevolence.

Barb, a friend of the family who was instrumental in organizing fund-raisers said, "I remember selling many tickets. We were worried about having enough cookies for the desserts but family, friends, co-workers, church members and people from the surrounding communities got involved and we had cookies coming out our ears! We had a barn dance, auction and the barbecue in Jenera where the building was full most of the night."

"What I remember most was all the monetary donations through the mail from people who had known the Core family over the years," she added. "The notes were so uplifting. People would often say they wished they could do more. It truly proved that a little from all adds up in a hurry. Over and over again, it was about the relationships in life that are made little by little and have a lasting impact on others. Amy's bravery and fight for life is one of those lessons remembered by all who knew her. The gift of lungs from a stranger and the prayers from many kept Amy going."

The World's Best Mom

Erica was the anchor who held Amy to life. From the moment her daughter was born, Amy celebrated being a Mom and played an active role in supporting Erica's participation in school activities and athletic events.

In 1999, Amy and Terry purchased a home in Arlington, Ohio where Erica started first grade. This was a good move for the entire family. They enjoyed living in the small community, and Erica quickly made new friends at school.

Erica's memories of elementary school are positive ones because Amy was at each event. One fond memory was being in an 'alphabet play' for parents and guests. The children were required to dress like the alphabet letter they were given and recite a short verse. Erica ended up with the letter 'Z' somehow, which meant a creative challenge lay ahead.

Even though Amy didn't sew well, she was determined to make Erica's costume. Many hours of labor were involved as Amy sewed a large 'Z' on the front of a black dress and attached zippers to it. Erica loved wearing her costume in the play and recited her verse perfectly. Amy was arguably the proudest Mom in the audience that day.

Erica especially enjoyed playing soccer in elementary school. Amy enjoyed watching her play even more. This was evident to everyone in attendance as she cheered loudly for the team. Without hesitation she voiced her feelings when Erica was on the bench and clearly let the referees know when she disagreed with their calls.

By the time Erica played volleyball and softball in junior high and high school, something had to be done to tone down Amy's vociferous enthusiasm at the ballgames. She was asked to keep statistics for the team and sit on the bench with the girls. This was a winning situation for everyone. Amy could no longer express her opinions to the referees and the girls enjoyed being with her.

Terry loved surprising Amy with flowers or clothes. Although Amy loved being spoiled, she was watchful of the money and frequently reminded him to stop spending so much on her. Finally, he started removing the price tags. Even when Amy specifically asked Erica how much money he'd spent, Erica just smiled. She and her dad were bound to secrecy.

Amy and Erica truly were best friends. Erica looked forward to coming home from school and telling her mother about her day. Whenever Amy was hospitalized, Erica would crawl into the hospital bed with her and share what was happening in her daily life. Throughout the years, Terry took many pictures of them together in hospital beds. Despite feeling ill so often, Amy smiled in every picture when Erica was beside her.

What follows are some of the stories Erica wrote in elementary school about her two favorite people.

My Family

My family is pretty cool. My mom has lung problems and has to go to the doctor a lot. We still have a lot of fun. Our whole family gets together every Sunday after church. Thanks for letting me share things about my family.

November 17, 2003

The World's Best Mom

I think that my mom is the world's best mom. I think she is because she made it through a lot of hard things. She has made it through a double lung transplant. She has made it through pneumonia a lot. She has almost died a couple of times. But she is alive.

December 16, 2003

The World's Best Dad

The world's best dad is my dad. He helps me through a lot of things. Sometimes he can spoil me a lot. He helps a lot when my mom is sick. This is why my dad is the world's best Dad.

January 14, 2004

The Best Time in My Life

The best time in my life was when my mom lived. I picked that because I was so thankful. She was so close to dying. I love her and I don't want her to die. My family didn't want her to die either. That was the best time in my life.

January 15, 2004

The Bumper Sticker

Two years after the transplant, the doctors were pleased for the most part with how well Amy's body adapted to the new lungs and the anti-rejection medications. However, she began having kidney problems within one year of the transplant due to high doses of antibiotics that were prescribed to ward off lung infections. As time progressed, there was permanent kidney damage. In the doctors' minds, Amy was often one step away from needing dialysis.

In the fall of 2003, Amy developed a serious lung infection that required hospitalization at Blanchard Valley Hospital. Unfortunately, none of the prescribed antibiotics worked and Dr. Watson made the decision to have Amy transported by ambulance from Findlay to Loyola University Medical Center.

This came as no surprise to Terry and Amy. They knew she was very ill by her shortness of breath and deep coughing. They arrived at Loyola on a Friday and realized that her specialists wouldn't be working on a weekend. They thought the medical staff would determine she had pneumonia and would prescribe potent antibiotics. This time, however, there were other infections involved that the doctors weren't sure how to treat. One doctor took Terry aside and told him to contact family members. At that point, the medical staff didn't think Amy would live through the weekend.

Terry didn't tell Amy what the doctor advised. He knew she would tell him not to call family members because she continued to believe she would beat the infections. Terry thought she could, too. He was taken aback, however, when he saw her connected to all types of hoses and breathing tubes. Amy looked gravely ill and appeared to be worse than she was during the transplant. Terry called Bob and let him make the decision whether to contact the entire family.

Erica was sitting on the couch at Bob and Leona's when her dad called. Leona answered and Terry immediately asked to speak to Bob. Erica knew it was very bad news. When her grandpa hung up the phone, he began to cry.

Cathy was working with the yearbook staff at school when an office aide said her father was on the phone. It had to be devastating news. Bob had never called Cathy in the middle of the day her entire life, much less in the middle of a school day.

When Cathy picked up the phone, her father said, "You need to get to Chicago. Amy's bad."

The conversation ended there. Cathy quickly called her husband, Jim and told him they needed to leave for Chicago right away. Even though Cathy realized that Amy was barely clinging to life, she believed Amy would find the strength to beat the medical odds like she had done so many times in her life.

Cathy and Jim were the last to arrive at Loyola. Red eyes and wadded-up tissues were a prelude to more bad news. Amy's infection was worse and the family had been told that none of the antibiotics were working. The doctors said there was nothing more they could do.

When it was Cathy and Jim's turn to go into Amy's room, Jim started sobbing when he saw Amy lying so still and lifeless. He walked over to the side of the bed and tried to crawl in beside her hoping to somehow comfort her fragile body and spirit. Cathy held her sister's hand and said, "Amy, we love you and we know you can beat this."

Saturday was a blur for the 18-member family who took over one section of the waiting room. The only information they were given the entire day was that further tests were being run. On Sunday morning, they congregated in a private conference room. They were praying that Terry would deliver some encouraging news. Instead the news was grim. None of the test results looked good and the medications were not working. It was only a matter of time until they would lose Amy.

Leona broke down and Bob looked defeated. After the tears subsided, plans had to be made. Who would stay in Chicago with Amy and Terry and who would return home? The final decision was for Cathy and Jill to stay. Bob and Leona would return home and take care of Erica.

As Jill and Cathy told their families goodbye, Bob walked over to Cathy and quietly but firmly said, "I want you to bring her home. Whether she lives or dies, bring Amy home."

The two sisters awoke early Monday morning and called the

administrators at their respective schools with lesson plans. Cathy then phoned Jim to talk with him before he left the house with their daughter, Jessica. When he didn't answer, she tried reaching him at his mother's house. Even though Jim wasn't there, Cathy's mother-in-law wanted to talk to her.

Cathy was in a hurry to leave for the hospital, but her mother-in-law was determined to talk. She told Cathy that she had been praying for Amy all weekend. She felt like Jesus was telling her that He would heal Amy if the sisters would ask. Jim's mother told Cathy she needed to physically hold Amy's hand and ask Jesus to heal her. Cathy assured her that she would. After sharing with Jill what her mother-in-law had said, Cathy didn't give the conversation another thought.

More bad news awaited them at the hospital. The doctors had tried another combination of antibiotics that didn't seem to be working. They had sent more of Amy's lab tests to be analyzed and it would be hours or perhaps days before they learned the results.

Although Amy was extremely weak, she tried to smile when her sisters arrived. Jill and Cathy chattered back and forth to keep the awkward silence out of the room. In her heart Cathy knew she should follow her mother-in-law's advice. In her mind she kept thinking that God already knew she wanted Him to heal Amy. Why did she need to ask?

When Cathy suggested to Jill that they pray aloud, Jill jumped up from her chair. While Cathy held Amy's left hand and foot, Jill held her right hand and foot. They asked Jesus over and over to heal Amy. The prayer lasted a matter of minutes. Later that day, the nurses delivered some good news. Amy's fever had gone down slightly. By Wednesday, the two sisters were praying each time they came into Amy's room and each time they left. When they prayed, "Jesus, please heal Amy," they received good news from the doctors.

Then they experienced their miracle. The doctors said Amy's test results were in and the antibiotic cocktail they had administered was working. They said she had progressed so much that she could possibly go home Friday. Jill and Cathy headed back to the hotel to call their families and pack their bags.

Jill had become very adept at maneuvering through Chicago traffic with the help of Cathy's back seat driving. As they came to a stoplight, Cathy encouraged her sister to pass a large van so they wouldn't be situated where they couldn't see the stoplights ahead.

Jill passed the van and two stoplights later, the same van was once again in front of them. The sisters gasped simultaneously when they saw the van's bumper sticker that read: 'Jesus heals-Just Ask!'

For Cathy, this was a testament that God has tremendous patience with oblivious people. She believed that He not only put the bumper sticker where she could see it, but He put it there a second time so she wouldn't miss the message.

Throughout that week, Karen was home and desperately worried that Amy would die. These fears multiplied when she didn't receive a phone call from anyone in the family. When she couldn't stand it any longer, she called Amy's cell phone.

When Terry answered, Karen's voice quivered when she asked, "Is Amy still with us?"

Terry calmly said, "She's doing better now, Karen. Would you like to talk to her?"

In profound disbelief, Karen said, "Do you mean I can actually talk to her?"

Terry handed Amy the phone and a very weak voice whispered, "Hi, Karen. I had a long talk with God last night and told Him I wasn't ready to go yet."

What follows are the two emails that Lisa and Deb sent to relatives and friends. They wanted everyone to know that Amy had beaten the medical odds once again.

Wednesday, September 24, 2003 10:21 a.m.

We are so grateful to God and all our friends for answered prayers. Amy is improving. Cathy and Jill are staying in Chicago for the remainder of the week. They reported home last night that Amy will be getting a blood transfusion today due to her hemoglobin count being off. The doctors have also detected another 'bug' in her system. Both of these issues are not uncommon for Amy and at this time we do not view them as setbacks.

The good news is that she gained a couple of pounds in the last two days. This is great because she lost so much weight these past several weeks. When talking on the phone with Amy yesterday, her voice sounded stronger than the day before. She continues to gather strength each day and yesterday she was up and waiting for her sisters to give her a shower and wash her hair. Overall, Amy is facing a long recovery, but she is determined to beat the infection.

Thanks for the prayers and special thoughts. They are providing an enormous amount of strength to Amy during these difficult days.

Lisa and Deb

Friday, September 26, 2003 1:43 p.m.

Hallelujah and Praise the Lord! As a family, we have been holding our breath all week. It has finally come true. Amy was dismissed from the hospital in Chicago this morning and is on her way home! We are so very excited, thankful and nervous. The test results on the CMV infection also came back 'negative' late yesterday which is one less thing to worry about and the one issue that would have kept Amy in the hospital longer.

Some of you may be wondering how this can be. Well, this is not an uncommon practice for Amy to come home even though she is still very ill. There will be home health nurses visiting her daily for awhile and she will continue to be ever so careful to avoid being around others who have colds or other maladies because her immune system is even weaker now. As we all know, it is far easier to recuperate at home than it is in a hospital and all the germs associated with it.

We truly appreciate all the prayers and support everyone has provided Amy and the family these past few weeks. We know that it is through the power of prayer and Amy's determination that she is able to come home so soon. Please continue to keep her in your prayers. Amy still has weeks of recovery in front of her. She must continue to battle the infection, get stronger and gain weight.

Thanks so very much to our friends and family.

Lisa and Deb

The Camping Trip

When Amy was hospitalized at Loyola University Medical Center in the fall of 2003, the medical staff predicted she would die within a limited number of days. Somehow, Amy's body and spirit joined forces and revived her when she was seemingly down to her last breath. Amy's ability to recover from this close encounter with death was miraculous. As unbelievable as it seemed, Amy had the physical stamina to go camping for four days in the summer of 2004.

Amy and Cathy decided they were up to the challenge of taking all the nieces on a camping adventure in Cathy's pop-up camper. Due to previous commitments, none of the other aunts could volunteer to spend that much outdoor time with the eight giggling, guy-gawking girls.

These sisters were the perfect duo to chaperone the excursion. They were easy-going and free-spirited personalities who always found a way to have fun and never have much of an agenda. Whether it was throwing a Frisbee in the campground driveway, playing putt-putt or going to the pool to check out the cute lifeguard, Amy and Cathy didn't get excited about following a plan. They did, however, enjoy delegating responsibilities with pretended authority. Consequently, the girls were given assignments. Some were in charge of cooking while others were in charge of cleaning up and keeping the campfire going to roast marshmallows.

At night, most of the girls wanted to sleep in the comfortable camper. Amy and Erica, however, chose to sleep in the tent. Although it was hot at night, these two wouldn't sleep in the air-conditioned camper. (There was a rumor that Aunt Cathy was quite the 'snorer' and Erica was a light sleeper who couldn't handle the noise.) No matter the reason, Amy and Erica snuggled in their sleeping bags and spent three nights on the ground with a fan blowing on them to

71

keep the mosquitoes away.

There wasn't anything one wouldn't do for the other. If Amy looked hot, Erica picked up something to fan her. If Erica wanted to play a game of cards, Amy was grabbing and shuffling the deck of cards. This mother and daughter instinctively looked after each other. They also respected one another's need for personal space. Amy knew that Erica needed her cousins like Amy needed her sisters; times like these were bonding memories.

At the time no one really looked at the camping trip as something special. No one really thought about the camping trip as possibly being Amy's last. Everyone was simply camping and busy making fun of each other's inability to cook, fear of spiders and hatred of dirty public shower houses.

The joy was in the moment, and Amy knew better than anyone else how to make this happen. She often coughed so hard that it took her breath away. Occasionally, someone might look at her with concern if the coughing went on too long, but for the most part, the girls took Amy's illness in stride. Amy relished playing the part of mother and aunt, even when the temperature and humidity played havoc with her health.

Family Vacations

Most people look forward to that time in their lives when they can retire. The thought never occurred to Bob. Instead, he was doing roof repairs on his barn at the age of 70. In his mind, 'retirement' meant 'stop working.' This was something he didn't know how to do. The only breaks he took were at 6 a.m. and 4 p.m. daily when he jumped in his truck, drove a few miles down the road and had a cup of coffee at 'the station' with his farming buddies. Even though the gas pumps were no longer in service at this small, iconic convenience store, the camaraderie was enjoyed, the jokes were expected and the friendships were genuine.

Each Wednesday morning, Leona went to 'the station' to share a cup of coffee and warm laughter with her friends. When this ritual began, the ladies decided to add a feminine touch to 'the station' and renamed it the 'Cory-Rawson Café.' This gathering place became the women's refuge for therapy and goodwill. This is where loyal friends gathered to support one another in every possible way.

When Leona announced to Bob that she was retiring and would no longer be helping with farming, he finally gave retirement some serious thought. At age 73, he asked his neighbor to farm his ground. Once Bob made the decision, he didn't change his mind. Even though he continued to oversee the farm operation, it was difficult for him to step back and no longer be the sole caretaker.

Bob turned his energy towards helping his daughters and their families with major home remodeling projects. Instead of relaxing, he spent endless hours in his shop building Christmas gifts for his daughters and granddaughters. Nothing pleased him more than to see the appreciation in his daughters' eyes when they unwrapped beautiful pieces of furniture, wall clocks and curio cabinets. Nothing pleased him more than the smiles on his

73

granddaughters' faces when they unwrapped their toy boxes, jewelry boxes and mini clocks. What Bob and Leona appreciated most about being retired, though, was the opportunity to attend all their granddaughters' school and athletic events. When Bob joined Leona at a granddaughter's piano recital, his daughter was stunned. So was everyone else in the audience.

In the summer of 2001, Bob and Leona invited their family to join them at Disney World in Florida. The granddaughters were at a perfect age to enjoy the whimsical adventure and so were the adults. When the gates opened to this enchanting kingdom, Amy headed for the fastest and wildest rides she could find. Bob was right behind his thrill-seeking daughter. When he buckled himself in for 'The Tower of Terror' ride, he didn't realize it was appropriately named. Bob soon learned.

Leona delighted in seeing her granddaughters' eyes sparkle when they had breakfast with the Disney characters and posed for pictures with them. This fun vacation had been about being together. It had been about celebrating Amy's stamina to embrace every minute of the magic.

There were tornado warnings the day the families traveled to the Orlando Airport to return home. As dark clouds circled overhead on a warm afternoon, Leona was visibly afraid for her family's safety. Thirty minutes passed and right before they were called to board the plane, Leona exclaimed, "There's a rainbow! Grandma is smiling and is with us in spirit." The dark clouds disappeared and so did Leona's fears.

In 2006, it was time for the Core clan to pack their bags again. They were all going to Hawaii to celebrate Bob and Leona's fiftieth wedding anniversary. This would be a trip filled with sweet memories, especially for Bob and Leona. They realized how blessed they were as a family.

When they arrived in Maui, everyone was exhausted from the long flight. They couldn't afford being tired too long, though, because they were about to experience days of extraordinary sight-seeing and a snorkeling excursion. Bob was especially looking forward to seeing Pearl Harbor.

While a few of the families chose to catch up on sleep their first morning on the island, Bob and Leona awoke during the twilight hours. They were going with Deb, Cathy and Jill's families to the top of Haleakala Mountain where they witnessed the breathtaking splendor of God's sunrise.

Amy and Lisa's families drove along the shore and took turns venturing down the rocks to see the bright cascade of fish in the crystal clear water. Amy and Erica enjoyed standing as close to the edges of the cliffs as possible, while Terry strongly encouraged his fearless wife and daughter to step back.

The snorkeling trip was pure adventure. As their boat journeyed further from shore, everyone was captivated by the entertaining dolphins which momentarily helped Leona forget how afraid she was swimming in deep water. She was determined, however, to set her fears aside by tightening her life jacket, getting on a boogie board and floating in the ocean with her family. Everyone was so proud of her when she put her face in the water and was spellbound by the parade of fish that reflected every color of the rainbow.

As this wonderful vacation was nearing an end, Terry had been busy planning an anniversary surprise for the honored couple. He first found a secluded beach on the north side of the island that set the perfect mood for a romantic dinner. The second phase of his plan involved renting a Subaru Outback wagon that he loaded with a plastic table, two chairs, plates, silverware and wine goblets.

As the memorable celebration began, Terry had Bob and Leona hold hands as they walked to their private table that was decorated with a linen tablecloth and a vase holding a single red flower. Leona wore a chartreuse blouse and lei, while Bob sported a Hawaiian shirt. As the newlyweds of fifty years were seated, their family transformed into waiters and waitresses who served a fine meal of steak, rice and cheesecake, topped off with a bottle of champagne and a cigar for Bob. Leona wanted to preserve this beautiful moment by having their granddaughters pose with them for pictures that she later had made into Christmas cards.

This nostalgic night was a perfect ending to a perfect vacation tinged with melancholy. Amy's lungs were becoming increasingly weaker, and although no one knew it outside of his immediate family, Bob's health was seriously deteriorating. Even though Amy and Bob never complained once about not feeling well, everyone knew this was the last vacation they would ever spend together as a family.

The Proud Farmer

Bob's health had been deteriorating from polycythemia, a disorder of the bone marrow that primarily causes excess production of red blood cells. Often, excess white blood cells and platelets are produced as well. This rare disease occurs more often in men than women, and the exact cause is unknown. The goal of treatment is to reduce the thickness of the blood to prevent bleeding and clotting.

Bob had been living with this disease for over twenty years and dealt with several of the symptoms which included weakness and fatigue, itchy skin, redness in the skin, especially the face, excessive bleeding and bruising and an enlargement of the spleen that he eventually had removed.

When Bob was diagnosed in 1985, his daughters were young adults. Even though he assured them he would live a long life, this was the first time in the girls' lives that they realized their dad could die. It was unimaginable. They depended on him to always be there.

In June of 2007, the sisters were sitting outside on a Sunday afternoon with their parents while Bob reminisced about the trip to Hawaii. He then told the girls he had recently been examined by a specialist in Columbus. The doctor said there was nothing more they could do to manage his disease. By now, he had lost a great deal of weight and had no energy. Even though his daughters knew this disease would one day take his life, they were in denial. Their dad was the family's pillar of strength.

Jill was sitting in the doctor's waiting room with Bob in July when he said, "Jill, I've lived a good life. I'm ready to die. What kind of life is it when I get down on my knees to work and can't get up?"

On August tenth, Bob mowed the yard before being admitted to the hospital with four bleeding ulcers. Although he immediately received a blood transfusion to improve the blood platelet levels, the doctors told the family if the platelet count didn't go up, there was nothing left to do but request hospice care.

Bob's blood platelet levels did not improve and his health

declined dramatically. He was dismissed from the hospital on August 20th and received hospice care at home. After being home ten days, he had a lengthy discussion with the two neighbors who farmed his ground. Although he was very weak and tired, Bob didn't let on how little energy he had while the men discussed the wheat prices, keeping the fence rows clean and the crops that would be planted in the fall. As the neighbors were leaving, Bob thanked them for taking good care of his ground. He also made a point to let them know how much he valued their friendship.

Afterwards, Deb and Terry helped Bob to the bathroom. Within minutes of getting him settled comfortably back in bed, Bob passed away. Twenty minutes earlier, he had been joking with the neighbors. Deb put things in perspective when she said, "I guess Dad had some business to finish before he passed."

Bob wanted "Amazing Grace" sung at his funeral. Amy, Jill and Deb sang it beautifully for their dad. Leona grieved for the only man she had ever loved, the man who stopped along the country roads to pick wildflowers for his sweetheart.

More Concerns

In July of 2008, Leona mentioned to her daughters that she didn't feel well. She was tired all the time and often felt like she wasn't thinking clearly. The girls attributed part of this to the medication she was put on one month earlier for a blood clot in her leg. They also attributed part of it to Leona's depression from Bob's death and Amy's deteriorating health.

When Leona wasn't feeling better by late September, her daughters insisted that she see the doctor. Following one of the several tests the doctor ordered, Leona was told she had a lump in her breast. The biopsy results indicated a malignancy. She didn't tell her family for a number of days as she tried to cope with the reality of having cancer.

For Leona's 71st birthday, Lisa had a Sunday brunch for the entire family. When Leona and her daughters were sitting together at the table, she told them she had breast cancer. The sisters were stunned and concerned for her physical and emotional well-being. They had her contact a surgeon immediately, and she underwent a lumpectomy in mid-December. Even though Amy was on oxygen every day, coughing a great deal and unable to walk very far, she was determined to be with her mother and sisters for Leona's oncology appointments.

The oncologist recommended a series of radiation treatments that started in early January and finished in March. The treatments would have ended sooner, but Leona rescheduled some of them when Amy became extremely ill in mid-January.

The Perilous Drive

In the spring of 2007, Amy and Terry were greatly concerned when they learned that Amy's insurance plan was no longer accepted by Loyola University Medical Center. Consequently, they immediately began to look at other prominent medical centers that would accept her insurance coverage. Ultimately, they decided to have her medical records transferred to the University of Michigan Hospital in Ann Arbor, which was only a ninety-minute drive from their home. By the spring of 2008, Amy was under their care when a team of pulmonary specialists treated her for a lung infection.

Early in the evening on January 14, 2009, Amy called both Leona and Lisa and said, "I don't feel good. We're going to Ann Arbor tomorrow." In the past, there were times when Amy felt ill but delayed going to the hospital in fear of picking up more germs and viruses. She was also mindful of incurring more medical expenses. This time was different. Amy wanted to get to Ann Arbor as soon as possible.

When they left home at eight o'clock the next morning, the weather conditions couldn't have been worse. The highways were covered with snow and ice. Terry was petrified of being in an accident on the way. Amy kept telling him to drive faster, but he couldn't. He was paranoid about losing control and sliding into the ditch.

The road conditions were so treacherous that the drive to Ann Arbor took four hours. Although Terry had packed four hours of extra oxygen, he had to continually turn up the levels because Amy was struggling to breathe. He was terrified they wouldn't get to the hospital in time. As they got closer to Ann Arbor, Amy started crying. She felt like she was suffocating which meant her blood wasn't absorbing enough oxygen.

Terry had alerted the hospital they were coming, and the

medical team was standing by when they arrived. Even though Amy became ill so quickly, she'd gone through traumatic spells like this before and responded well to the medications and treatments. They both hoped that she would only be in the hospital ten to twelve days based on previous experiences. These hopes were never realized. Instead, Amy and Terry were about to face the biggest nightmare of their lives.

Courage

During Amy's extensive stay in the hospital, Lisa kept detailed notes that she emailed to family members and friends who were praying for Amy to survive. Everyone sensed the urgent need for prayer. Amy was so gravely ill that her frail body was saying, "I can't endure this suffering anymore," while her courageous spirit was saying, "I can still endure."

Friday, January 16, 2009

Calling all prayer warriors.

On January 7ᵗʰ, Amy had a doctor's appointment in Findlay because she wasn't feeling well. At that time, x-rays did not show any problems with her lungs. Doctors thought she might have the flu and prescribed an antibiotic. She continued to feel worse and on January 14ᵗʰ, she contacted her doctors in Ann Arbor and asked them to admit her. After tests were run, they found pneumonia in the lower right lobe and administered two strong antibiotics. She was moved to ICU today and a breathing tube has been inserted. She is heavily sedated and is sleeping a lot. When I talked to her on the 14ᵗʰ, she hadn't had much sleep over the last five to six days, had severe headaches and was coughing a lot. I am praying for her weak body to fight back as she weighs around 110 pounds.

Please keep Amy in your prayers.

Saturday, January 17, 2009

Terry said Amy rested well last night. Jill, Brad and I went to see her today. She was awake in the morning for a little bit but couldn't talk due to the breathing tube. We didn't visit long but she knew we were there. She is heavily sedated to reduce movement. Terry said they are going to take it day by day. Erica is at the hospital with him. Deb and

Mom are going to see Amy tomorrow.

Thank you for your continued prayers.

Sunday, January 18, 2009

According to Deb, there is no real change in Amy's condition. Her color is good. She opened her eyes and knew Mom and Deb were in the room. Deb told Amy that everyone is praying for her and Amy acknowledged Deb by blinking her eyes. Amy was moved to the ICU pulmonary unit on the sixth floor. This is good because she is with pulmonary specialists.

The doctor said it will be at least a week before they take out the breathing tube and she will be heavily sedated for that time. She may need a blood transfusion tomorrow. Erica and Terry are in Ann Arbor this evening. We are returning to the hospital tomorrow and will bring Erica home so she can return to school on Tuesday.

Thank you for your continued prayers.

Monday, January 19, 2009

Early this morning, Amy was awake for awhile and Terry said she was a little feisty which was a good sign. On Friday when she was hooked up to the breathing tube, the ventilator was doing 100 percent of the work. Today, the machine was doing 40 percent of the work.

The doctors are monitoring the pressure of air in her lungs which is called PEEPS. On Friday, the number was ten; today she is at eight and the doctors want her at five. They are very concerned about how anemic Amy is and started giving her blood transfusions this afternoon. They are also concerned that her kidneys are not responding or functioning as well as they had hoped. The drugs Amy takes do affect the kidneys. There is nothing more to say other than we look to the doctors to help Amy and pray to God to provide His healing power. Terry remains in Ann Arbor and is staying at a motel.

Thank you for your continued prayers.

Karen came to see Amy the Monday after she was moved to the intensive care unit with pneumonia. When she arrived, Terry was waiting for her outside Amy's room. There was a sound of desperate fear in his voice when he said nothing had gone as they hoped. He never anticipated that Amy would be fighting for her life.

When Karen walked into Amy's room, Erica was holding her mother's hand. Karen reached for Amy's other hand and reminded her friend how much everyone was praying for her. Unable to talk, Amy smiled. When Erica left the room for a few minutes, Karen leaned over, kissed Amy on the forehead and said, "Amy, I am so proud of you for all the fighting you've done your whole life. If you are ready to let go, then let go. God is here for you. If you are strong enough to keep fighting, I hope you fight."

When Amy lightly squeezed Karen's hand, Amy was saying, "I'm going to fight."

Sunday, January 25, 2009

Amy had limited support with the ventilator today. Her lungs were doing most of the work and the ventilator would kick in when needed. She did this for about three hours. She was very tired afterwards and received pain killers and more sedatives to help her sleep. Her body is weak. She still has the tubes in her nose, one feeding her and the other suctioning the mucus from her lungs. She communicates by writing down her thoughts.

Thank you for your continued prayers.

Tuesday, January 27, 2009

Amy had two surgeries today. The doctors inserted a tracheotomy in her neck that will make it easier for her to breathe. They removed the breathing tube from her throat and the tube from the nostrils that suctioned out the mucus. All of these tubes are now hooked up to the tracheotomy. The doctors adjusted the ventilator to support 50 percent of the breathing to help Amy rest.

The second surgery involved inserting a PEG which means the feeding tube has been moved from her nostrils to her stomach. The doctor thought it was best to get the tubes out of her throat and away from her face. The hope is that she will be able to have liquids and regular food soon. However, her throat will need time to heal.

While Amy was in surgery, the doctors moved the IV line from her right arm to her left one because her right arm was starting to turn purple. She is again sedated to sleep comfortably. We are hopeful these procedures help Amy as the doctors highly recommended this aggressive approach to help her heal.

The following Bible verse was shared with us today that we'd like to pass on as you continue to pray for Amy: "But if it were I, I would appeal to God; I would lay my cause before Him. He performs wonders that cannot be fathomed, miracles that cannot be counted." Job 5:8-9

Although the tracheotomy procedure had been successful, Amy was extremely disappointed when she lost her voice for nearly three weeks. She would mouth what she wanted and it was often difficult to understand her questions. Most of the time, she communicated by writing her thoughts on paper. When she talked on the phone with her family and they asked her questions, she would tap a pencil once for 'yes' and twice for 'no.'

At this point, it was time for Terry to renew their family cell phone contract. He purchased a phone with a texting feature that enabled Amy to stay in close touch with her family and friends. Lisa, who had recently purchased the same phone, spent the day with her while they tried to figure out how to use them. Through Amy mouthing her ideas and Lisa asking her to write down what she was saying, they had a full day. Lisa encouraged her to relax about losing her voice and told her it would return before she knew it.

Lisa left the hospital with a heavy heart. As she walked to the parking garage, she prayed for her sister. About fifteen minutes south of Ann Arbor, Lisa's cell phone rang. When she answered, it was Amy saying, "My voice...I can talk, Lisa! I'm going to call everyone else and let them know my voice is back. The nurses said my voice will come and go. I want to talk to everyone before I lose my voice again!"

With tears sliding down her face, Lisa said, "Go for it, Amy! I love you." Later that evening, Amy sent Lisa a text that she had lost her voice again.

When it became obvious that Amy was not going to be leaving the hospital for quite awhile, Terry started driving back and forth to Ann Arbor daily. Erica spent the weekends with Amy, and her sisters and Leona made frequent trips to Ann Arbor. By this time, Leona was so tired from her radiation treatments that her daughters would transport her in a wheelchair to Amy's room. During one of the visits, Lisa and Leona washed Amy's hair. Somehow she garnered the strength to sit in a chair and lean over the small sink while protecting her tracheotomy tube.

Even though Amy's body tired easily, her mind and wit remained sharp. During one of Jill's visits with Amy, Jill mentioned that she and Mike needed to find someone to drive Mike's mother, Nancy to medical appointments following her hip surgery. Five years earlier, Amy, who was relatively healthy, volunteered to drive Nancy to various appointments. This arrangement worked well for the next few years. Amy enjoyed being able to help and Nancy appreciated the time spent with Amy.

As soon as Jill mentioned the need to find a driver for Nancy again, Amy mustered the strength to raise her hand and whisper, "I'll do it, Jill."

Jill, Deb and Lisa kept Cathy updated daily on Amy's condition. When Cathy first learned that Amy had been admitted to Ann Arbor, she thought Amy would pull through like she always had. Cathy and Leona were of the same mindset.

Two weeks after Amy was admitted to the hospital, Cathy came home for the weekend to visit her. Even though everyone in the family had described Amy's grave condition, nothing prepared Cathy for the tubes and equipment that surrounded the thin, pale image of her sister lying in the hospital bed. Amy had never looked so fragile. Upon seeing Cathy, she managed a weak, little grin. Although the grin might have been small, it was mighty in Cathy's eyes. Amy still had spirit and spunk.

Cathy was impressed with Amy's determination to understand her medical care and her ability to communicate her concerns to the medical staff. Even though the tracheotomy made it so difficult for her to talk, she didn't hesitate to question doctors, nurses and therapists about her treatments and medications.

Amy hated how her situation was affecting everyone's daily lives. Cathy joked with Amy that her visit was just an excuse to spend time with their mother and convince Leona that 'she' was her favorite child, not Amy. All their lives, these two sisters loved teasing one another. In her choppy, raspy voice, Amy said, "Cathy, the joke is on you because Mom doesn't even like you."

Wednesday, February 11, 2009

Amy has now been in the hospital four weeks. Her doctor had hoped to be able to let her go home by now. At this point, we don't have a defined time when she will be released. She is experiencing anxiety attacks when they try to gradually wean her off the ventilator. Her lung infection is still being fought with three antibiotics. Hopefully, there will be good results. If not, they'll try different antibiotics.

Please continue to keep Amy in your prayers. Pray for her to gain some strength and to gradually get off the ventilator. Amy's doctor told her that she needs to be able to be off the ventilator an entire day before she can go home.

Monday, March 16, 2009

Amy has had some setbacks with weaning herself off the ventilator. Terry is working with the caseworker to get a ventilator set up at home and is being trained in tracheotomy care.

Amy has a routine for every waking hour to stand up, move her arms, and tackle rubber band exercises to strengthen her arms and legs. The doctors have discovered a new virus in the lower right lobe of her lung and have started administering strong antibiotics. The doctors are monitoring her kidneys very closely while she is on antibiotics for at least another eight days.

Amy continues to express her gratitude for your prayers. Please pray for her lungs to grow stronger and for the new virus to be annihilated.

Monday, March 23, 2009

Amy successfully weaned herself off the ventilator by using the tracheotomy mask for five hours. Her doctor wants her to be able to function with the mask for eight hours before she can be released. Terry has the ventilator set up at home.

Terry and his brother, Brad are certified in tracheotomy care. They completed classes the past two weeks. With a nurse's guidance, they each practiced tracheotomy care on Amy.

Last Tuesday, Jill and Mom were able to wheel Amy outside with the assistance of John, Amy's nurse and physical therapist. She was thrilled to be out in the 67-degree weather and feel the warm sun. This Wednesday will mark the tenth week that she has been in the hospital.

Please pray for Amy to be able to wean to the trach mask for eight hours and to be able to go home within the next two weeks.

Monday, March 30, 2009

Awesome News!!! After 76 days in the hospital, Amy will be released at eleven a.m. tomorrow. She has been able to wean herself to the trach mask for seven hours and her kidney levels continue to be normal. She is gaining strength.

Terry and Brad have learned how to clean her tracheotomy, change and clean the air tubes, suction mucus from her lungs and read and set the ventilator machine. Terry has taken precautionary measures, and for backup power, a generator is at the house in the event of a spring storm interrupting electricity. The house has been thoroughly cleaned and sanitized. The company employees who trained Terry and Brad on the ventilator will be at the house when Amy arrives via ambulance to make sure all goes well with the ventilator machine.

Home health nurses will be present every day for an unknown period of time.

We are so very thankful to God and the blessings He has bestowed upon Amy. We are humbled by everyone's continued prayer and support. We pray for Amy's recovery at home as she faces an uphill climb to regain her strength.

Thank you and many blessings to all.

Lisa

During Amy's stay in the hospital, Amy and Terry were told by the doctors that her disease had decimated her lungs. There was nothing more they could do to prolong her life. Terry was determined to get Amy discharged from the hospital as soon as possible. No matter how many weeks or months Amy had to live, they wanted to spend that time at home as a family.

Amy's Support Team

Amy required 24-hour care. This meant Terry needed someone else to become certified in tracheotomy care to provide support. Initially, Lisa was going to take the training until her work schedule changed. At that point, Terry asked his brother, Brad to take the classes with him. Brad, who was laid off from his job, didn't hesitate and said, "Sure, I'll do whatever I can to help you and Amy."

In addition to being trained in the many areas of tracheotomy care, Terry and Brad also learned how to check Amy's heart rate, sugar level, blood pressure and oxygen saturation levels. Terry designed a chart that enabled him to record Amy's vitals.

During their training, Brad realized the medical staff didn't think he and Terry could learn everything in two weeks. In Brad and Terry's minds, they were certain they could, and they did. As Brad said, "Terry would have done whatever it took to bring Amy home. I don't know another man who could have taken care of his wife like my brother did. If that isn't love, I don't know what is."

Amy's first two weeks at home went well. In fact, it was hard slowing her down. Instead of resting after the ambulance transported her home, she immediately wanted to see her mother. This was the first of many trips when Terry and Brad would load her and the machines into the van. By the third day, she talked them into surprising Erica by picking her up after school. Every day Amy felt up to it, they took long rides.

Brad's presence was invaluable. Amy was very appreciative and thanked him each time he took care of her. In turn, Brad thanked Amy for the privilege of helping. More than once, he said, "Amy, it's an honor to take care of you. I made some bad decisions when I was younger. You're my redemption. I believe in God and know what faith means from watching you."

As soon as Amy arrived home from Ann Arbor, Terry was in close contact by phone with Dr. Watson. By the fourth week, she was growing visibly weaker and Terry had to suction mucus from her lungs with increasing frequency. Recognizing that she was failing day by day, Terry called Dr. Watson and asked for his honest opinion of Amy's condition.

Dr. Watson said, "Terry, when Amy was dismissed from the hospital at the end of March, her doctors in Ann Arbor gave her four to six weeks to live. There comes a point when nothing more can be done."

Terry paused and said, "I appreciate what you've done for Amy, Dr. Watson. You've always been upfront with us and we've had complete faith in you. Thank you."

Even though Amy and Terry knew the machines were doing all the breathing for her, they weren't prepared to hear so little time was left. Amy's goals changed that day. Her first goal was to see Erica turn sixteen years old at the end of July. Amy's second goal was to return to the ocean after Erica's birthday party. That night, Amy started a journal for Erica.

True Tenacity

Amy's last winter had been tough. She'd spent more than two months in the hospital. Her last spring was even tougher while she was basically confined to being at home. Every few weeks, Cathy would drive home to visit, thinking it would be the last time to see her sister. Amy had different plans. She looked weak and tired, but there was also this gleam in her eye when Cathy would sit next to her on the couch. One afternoon, Amy said, "Cathy, what are you doing here again? Did Debbie call you and tell you I was dying?" Cathy chuckled and said, "Yeah, what a worry-wart!" and their conversation resumed.

In late April, talk turned to preparations for the graduation party of Cathy's daughter, Jessica. Amy told Cathy she would be at the party. If that were to happen, Terry would need to load everything, travel for over three hours and stop frequently to suction the phlegm in Amy's lungs and tracheotomy tube.

Everyone else said not to entertain the idea of Amy making the trip. Cathy didn't. That changed, however, when Jessica received a birthday card on May 13th from Amy who wrote, "Happy Birthday- I WILL see you at graduation." Cathy's spirits were lifted because she knew Amy had set a goal to live another month. She knew Amy was determined to be part of the big day. Everyone thought it was a wonderful sentiment, but no one really believed Amy could do it. They didn't think she had the strength.

On graduation day, May 30th, Amy emerged from the van with Terry at her side and Lisa's husband, Brad at the wheel. It had taken more than four hours to make the trip. Cathy's friends, who had only heard of Amy and her ordeal, were amazed how she shared in the day's events.

Amy stayed the entire afternoon. If her oxygen hose twisted a certain way, the ventilator alarm beeped. The first time people heard it, they jumped in concern. That soon ended when they saw how calmly Amy reached over and pushed the 'stop' button. Cathy's friends also noticed that every time the alarm sounded, Terry sat up a little straighter, listening for the length of the beeping. When the sound stopped, his shoulders relaxed.

Cathy was overwhelmed that Amy would use so much of her precious energy to come to Jessica's graduation. That was Amy. She wanted to be part of the family gathering. For Cathy, her sister's efforts that day were life-time reminders how much Amy loved her entire family, and the extraordinary lengths she and Terry went to in order to make her life as normal as possible.

On the drive home, Brad looked in the rear-view mirror. As tears rolled down her cheeks, Amy stared sadly out the window. She knew this was her final trip to Cathy's house.

After Leona returned home from the graduation party, she first stopped at Lisa and Brad's before going to see Amy. When Lisa shared how emotional it had been for Amy to leave the party, Leona began to cry. Lisa hugged her and they cried together. Through her tears, Leona said, "A daughter should outlive her mother. This just isn't fair. I can't bury Amy."

Seafood and Yahtzee

When Leona was helping Cathy with the food preparation for Jessica's party, she mentioned that she had decided not to go with Lisa, Jill and Deb's families to Hilton Head the following week. She was concerned that Amy and Terry would be without help since Erica was going with everyone on the week-long vacation.

On Monday, Cathy pictured what a meaningful weekend it would be if she went to Ohio and spent one-on-one time with Amy and her mother. When Cathy shared her thoughts with Karen, her best friend and co-worker for twenty-five years, Karen was very much in favor of going. Leona was delighted when Cathy called to say they'd be arriving on June 5th and would stay the weekend.

Leona had supper ready as Cathy and Karen pulled into the driveway. Afterwards, they went to visit Amy, but didn't stay long because she was so tired.

Before leaving, Cathy said, "Amy, is there somewhere you'd like to eat tomorrow?"

"I can't go anywhere, Cathy. It's too much work to get there."

"I didn't say anything about taking you anywhere, Amy. Why can't I bring it to you?"

Amy smiled and said, "I'd like some crab legs but..."

"Nope! Don't worry. It's done. Amy, we'll see you tomorrow for supper."

The next morning involved a shopping trip. The lady behind the seafood counter was patient as Cathy surveyed the regular-sized crab legs and decided there weren't enough to suit her. Instead of sending her away disappointed, the lady rang up some larger crab legs at the same price as the smaller ones. Karen found the spices to boil the seafood delicacy, and they returned to Leona's feeling proud of their accomplishments. In the afternoon, they went to Deb's to plant flowers. Leona was able to offer little help, which was very uncharacteristic of her. Instead, she sat on the porch swing and mentioned how tired she was.

When the ladies arrived at Amy's that evening, they were

welcomed by Terry. He had set the mood for fine dining with a card table covered with a tablecloth and decorated with candles. The smell of baked potatoes circulated throughout the house, and a pot of boiling water awaited the crab legs.

They enjoyed hors d'oeuvres and iced tea before the feast began. Then Terry seated everyone and carried out a towel-covered tray of crab legs with steam rolling out the sides. He set the tray in front of Amy and whipped off the towel with a flourish. Her bright eyes and smile were proof of her delight.

Terry provided a pair of kitchen shears that made it easy to crack open the crab legs. They each grabbed one and started digging. Leona claimed she'd never eaten crab legs before and was a bit tentative until Amy showed her the tricks to getting the meat to come out in a hunk. Leona enjoyed every moment of this new dining experience. Everyone giggled as they dipped the huge hunks of crab in the butter. They ate nearly ten pounds of seafood and everyone there would have testified that Amy ate the biggest share.

After the table was cleared, the Yahtzee game began. Cathy explained to Karen that this was a family favorite going back to their childhood when they played it with their grandma. According to the legend, Grandma would toss a yahtzee in every game. Suddenly, everyone at the table tried to evoke Grandma's spirit. After playing a few intense rounds, Amy was getting tired, so her mother and sister kissed her goodnight.

As Cathy and Leona crawled into bed that night, they agreed the evening had been a success. They were happy to have been part of a meaningful memory for Amy. As they said their goodnights, they teased one another about keeping their snoring to a minimum.

The next morning, Cathy and Karen packed the van. Leona walked outside with them in her pajamas and housecoat.

"I'm not going to church today, Cathy. I'm tired."

"Mom, if you're tired, go to bed. We had a big day yesterday and you're probably still full from last night."

They laughed, they hugged and they kissed goodbye. This would be the last time Cathy would ever talk to her mother again.

The Paralyzing Phone Calls

On Saturday, June 6th, Lisa and her family rolled into the driveway on Heron Street and quickly jumped out of their vehicle after thirteen hours of driving. It was time to stretch, soak in the humid sunshine and enjoy the captivating atmosphere of Hilton Head Island. Lisa and her sisters had urged Leona to come with them, but her response was, "Would you take a vacation if your daughter was sick?"

It had been a difficult decision for everyone to leave Amy. When the rental contract for the beach house was signed in December of 2008, Amy's health appeared stable, despite her need to be on oxygen during the day and the constant coughing.

On Sunday, June 7th, at 5:55 in the evening, Lisa's inner voice said, "Call Mom to see how she's doing and to let her know we're thinking of her."

Leona sounded weary when she answered the phone.

"Hey, Mom, how are you doing?"

"I'm okay, Lisa. We had so much fun at Amy and Terry's. I've never laughed so much my entire life. I'm resting in bed now because I'm so tired."

"Okay, Mom, but will you please make an appointment with the doctor this week? We need to determine why you're so tired. Get some rest and we'll talk later. Love ya."

"Bye, Lisa."

Brad and Lisa were up early Monday morning to watch the 7 o'clock news and weather report. There was a 50 percent change of rain later that day, so they finished their cups of coffee and headed to the beach. As they spent a beautiful morning together looking for seashells, they were struck by the vibrant rainbow that clearly made its presence known. Brad pointed out a cloud in the shape of a teapot sitting ominously beside it, which proved to be a warning of temperamental weather coming their way. As they slowly walked back to the house, Brad and Lisa memorized the tranquility of the morning that was about to change.

95

The sisters and nieces opted to spend the afternoon shopping. At noon, Jill called her mother from the shopping mall, but there was no answer. Everyone assumed Leona was running errands. When they returned home, everybody was hungry. The sisters prepared supper and all the families ate together. As they were cleaning up the kitchen, Deb received a call on her cell phone. It was Terry. He asked how to get into Leona's house without breaking the screen door.

Everyone in the beach house stopped what they were doing. Hearts were pulsating in fear. Amy required Terry's constant care. This meant that he had called Brad to stay with Amy while he checked on Leona who hadn't returned his calls all day. Deb told him to break the door and call them back as soon as possible. As Terry felt the door breaking, so did his hopes. He had a sick feeling that something was terribly wrong. No one in the beach house said a word as the whirring of the ceiling fan ticked away seconds that felt like hours.

Terry called back twenty minutes later. He had found Leona in bed with her feet hanging over the side. He immediately called the EMS and lifted her legs onto the bed. Although she couldn't move, she squeezed Terry's hand when he said, "It's okay, Leona. Help is on the way."

As this tragedy unfolded, Cathy and her family were in Columbus, Indiana, buying a van. Cathy told the salesman she wanted automatic doors because her mother had difficulty with the ones on their previous van. As he pointed out a white one that met their requirements, Cathy laughed aloud. Most of Leona's vehicles in the past had been white. In Cathy's mind, this was a sign. They completed the paperwork and were pulling out of the parking lot in their white van when Cathy's cell phone rang.

There was no opportunity to say 'hello' before Deb said, "Cathy, what are you doing? How fast can you get home?"

By the panicked tone in Deb's voice, Cathy assumed the worst and thought Amy had passed away. When Deb explained Terry's phone call, it was beyond Cathy's comprehension how any of this could be real. As she quickly headed to Ohio, Deb called back with more information. According to the doctors and from what Terry could piece together, Leona had suffered a stroke sometime Sunday night. Although the details were still sketchy, Cathy feared a tragic, life-changing moment that would affect their family forever.

By 10 o'clock, Cathy had arrived at the hospital and was met by her cousin, Marvin and his wife, Linda who were standing outside Leona's ICU room. Linda said she thought Leona had responded to her voice and Terry's. The emergency room doctors painted a far graver picture. Leona had suffered a massive stroke, and the doctor advised Cathy to contact family members as soon as possible.

Cathy spent the night holding her mother's hand and pleading with her to wake up. Occasionally, Leona's hand would move or her foot would twitch. Cathy tried convincing herself that her mother heard her and was responding. This flicker of hope vanished when the doctor showed her the x-ray and pointed out the massive, dark area covering most of Leona's brain. She would never forget the chilling finality of those nine words when the doctor said, "Your mother will never come out of this coma."

There was nothing Cathy could do but grieve alone and hold her mother's hand. There was nothing she could do but wait for the fresh tears to fall when her sisters and their families arrived.

Fresh Tears

When Cathy called her sisters after talking with the doctor Tuesday morning, her voice quivered in sorrow. She could have never imagined a moment like this when she would have to say, "The stroke was massive. Mom will never come out of this coma."

The sisters and their families sobbed in despair and disbelief. Erica cried in fear for her mother, knowing this nightmare would be too devastating for Amy. Everyone began to pack quickly and quietly in preparation for the longest 14-hour drive of their lives. The sisters were in touch with Terry by phone so that he and Brad could have Amy at the hospital when everyone arrived. They wanted to be together to tell their mother goodbye.

"We spent our vacation with our mother, the person who loved us unconditionally our entire lives," Lisa sighed. "Mom was the most patient and giving woman I'll ever know. We are so proud to have been raised by a mother whose heart was filled with Christian love."

"I was grateful to be able to say goodbye to my mom," Jill shared. "It helped having her there when we got back. Knowing Mom wouldn't want the kind of life she was living made it easier to let her go. One of the most difficult things was watching Amy suffer. Amy had counted on Mom to be there for Erica."

Leona had been the one at Amy's side all her life to comfort her through many painful and depressing days. Now it was Amy sitting at her mother's bedside. Somehow, Amy found the strength to hold her mother's hand for hours. Somehow, Amy found the strength to say over and over, "It's okay, Mom."

Broken Heart

Journal Entry

June 12, 2009

I've just learned of Leona's death. I'm asking the same questions everyone else is asking: "Why did this happen, God? How much suffering can one family endure?"

The doctor said Leona died from a massive stroke. Family members and friends might say she also died of a broken heart that began to crumble when she and Bob were told Amy had cystic fibrosis. Leona's life was never the same after that. She awakened each morning to the cruel truth that it was only a limited number of years, months, weeks or days until Amy would lose the final battle.

God empowered Leona with a loving, maternal instinct. She knew when her children needed to be hugged, needed to feel safe and needed to hear her say, "You'll be okay. Things will get better."

Leona grieved silently, knowing she could never assure Amy that things would get better. She grieved when her daughter cried out in desperation to simply be like everyone else. How can a mother's heart not break when she knows she will likely bury the child she helped create?

Pieces of Leona's heart broke further when Bob died. They had raised a family together, built a farm operation together and weathered the tough times together. Bob's strong arms were no longer there to hold and comfort her.

Motherhood was a sacred blessing and treasured responsibility to Leona. She was thankful God chose her to be the mother of five daughters to whom she devoted her life. For Leona, being a mother was a privilege, a precious gift she handled with love and care.

Beyond Comprehension

Journal Entry

June 14, 2009

As I drove to the funeral home today, I tried to think of the right words to say. There are no right words to convey the depth of sorrow everyone is feeling for Bob and Leona's family. The tragedies they have suffered in such an incredibly short time seem surreal.

I walked into the funeral home with one of Jill's high school friends and her husband. We hugged and looked at one another in disbelief. This was a level of sadness beyond comprehension.

Within what seemed like seconds, I was shaking hands with Lisa and Brad who were the first family members in the receiving line. I enjoyed them so much in school and could visually recall where each one had sat. We hugged and Lisa said, "Beth, this is our daughter, Audrey."

Audrey was lovely. Standing beside her was another beautiful teenager. Lisa said, "This is Amy and Terry's daughter, Erica."

Tears could no longer be contained. Suddenly, I was looking at Amy's miracle, the child she had always dreamed of one day having.

As Erica extended her hand, I said, "My name is Beth Huffman, Erica. I adore your mother. She was my student in junior high, and I had the privilege of knowing your wonderful grandma." Erica then stepped to the side and said, "Here's Mom if you'd like to talk to her."

I hadn't been able to see Amy sitting on the small couch behind the family. I had assumed she was too ill to be at the funeral home. The moment our eyes met, I was reminded of the vivacious young girl who had changed my bulletin boards and my perspective on life. Amy tilted her head and smiled as I took a few steps forward, leaned over and gently touched her arm. She put her hand on top of mine. It was apparent by her pallor that the machines were breathing for her. I struggled to maintain my composure and said, "Amy, I'm so sorry you've lost your mother. I know you idolized her. You and Terry have such a beautiful daughter. I remember how you always talked about marrying a caring man and having a child someday."

As I stood up, Amy motioned for me to lean over again. She whispered, "Thank you so much for the bracelets you sent Erica and me. It meant so much."

I kissed my free spirit on the forehead and said, "You have always been my hero, Amy. You know that, don't you?"

As she nodded her head, a single tear slipped down her cheek. She patted my hand and whispered, "I know. Thank you, Beth."

I didn't have the opportunity to express my condolences to Terry because he had gone to the car to get another oxygen tank for Amy. The next thing I knew, I was hugging Cathy who introduced me to her husband, Jim, and their attractive daughter, Jessica. I knew in high school that Cathy would one day be the exceptional English teacher she is. I was able to tell her that as we hugged and I expressed my sympathy.

Deb was standing next to Cathy. With each sister, fond memories flashed through my mind. I had lunch with Deb several months after she brought her girls home. More tears gathered as Deb introduced me to her two darling daughters, Maria and Aly.

The last hug was for Jill. I couldn't look her in the eyes, so we hugged and cried together. I remember repeating, "I'm so sorry." I was flooded with memories of Amy being spellbound by Jill's portrayal on stage of Annie Sullivan. I remembered Leona's kind words and Bob's firm handshake after the show.

Jill and Mike's daughters, Kelsey, Devin and Blair, are such pretty girls. I told them how sorry I was they had lost their grandma who adored them. One of the girls said, "Our grandma loved all of us."

As I started to leave, I turned momentarily and looked at Bob and Leona's incredibly strong daughters who are exceptional mothers. They are carrying on Leona's legacy of motherhood. Although the daughters are collapsing emotionally, they are sturdy in humbly thanking everyone. Bob and Leona would be proud of their five girls. Bob and Leona would be so proud of their entire family.

Kindred Spirits Once More

Amy's friend, Barb has been in and out of the hospital frequently with lung complications and diabetes issues, the collateral damage of her cystic fibrosis. Throughout her own physical battles, Barb has been aware of Amy's declining health and her fight to live.

Barb visited Amy a few weeks prior to Leona's death. It was obvious then how tired Amy was and how difficult it was for her to breathe. When Barb saw Amy at Leona's visitation, she knew the end was near for her dear friend. She sat with Amy for a few hours at the funeral home and watched her eyes follow every step that Erica and Terry took. At one point, Terry changed Amy's oxygen tank and Amy looked at him and smiled. As Terry turned away, Amy had tears in her eyes and squeezed Barb's hand.

When it was time for Barb to leave, Amy held her hand and thanked her for coming. Through tear-filled eyes, Amy made sure she had Barb's full attention when she said, "Barb, you have to fight to live as long as you possibly can."

Barb and Joe visited Amy and Terry at the end of June when Amy was still feeling strong enough for company. Barb confided to Amy that her doctor had recently said she would need a lung transplant in two years if she continued regressing so quickly. The two friends talked about the risks of a transplant procedure and the required care afterwards. As she tried to ease Barb's fears, Amy answered her questions with honesty and clarity. Amy fervently reminded Barb that her lung transplant enabled her to spend eleven more years with Terry and Erica. Before Barb and Joe left, Amy wanted to share her final thoughts with her dear friend.

"Barb, I know you've always said you wouldn't go through a transplant. Once you are fighting for a breath, you will change your mind. You have to fight for your family who loves you."

Without hesitation, Barb said, "I know you're right, Amy."

After their visit, Barb cried most of the way home. When she and Joe stopped for dinner, Barb told him everything Amy had said. In turn, Joe shared what Terry told him was involved with the intense level of care required after a transplant.

Barb would never forget that day when Amy told her to have faith, to fight for life and to feel secure in knowing Joe would care for her like Terry cared for Amy. After that conversation, Amy convinced Barb to seriously consider a transplant. The moment these kindred spirits met as teenagers, Amy's inspirational attitude touched and changed Barb's life.

Blessings

Journal Entry

July 2009

In early July, Erica had the opportunity to participate in a Christian youth rally at Iowa State University with her cousin, Audrey and other youth group members from Audrey's church. Despite Amy's encouragement to go, Erica was naturally afraid to leave, especially since she was aware how much her mother's body and spirit had declined since Leona's death. Ultimately, the decision was made for Erica when Amy said, "You are going on this trip. It will be a great experience. I'm going to be right here when you get home."

Before leaving for the rally, Erica wrote an inspirational message on an erasable board. She set it at the end of the couch where Amy could comfortably read the words. The message was a reminder of Erica's love and admiration for her mother. The message was also a symbol of Amy's determination to keep pushing on through the pain and anguish.

By now, everyone knows that Amy's earthly journey is nearly over. Karen has been in frequent touch with Erica and Terry. Shortly after Leona's death, there was urgency in Amy's voice when she called Karen and asked her to come over. When Karen arrived, she wasn't prepared for the conversation that was about to take place. Amy wanted to say a final goodbye, and Karen wasn't ready to say those words. For several minutes, the two friends talked about Leona's death. Karen listened as Amy shared her grief.

"Karen, it wasn't supposed to happen this way. I was supposed to die, not my mom. I don't feel like I have any closure with her death. I'm so upset I can't physically go to the farm and look through her belongings. It just wasn't supposed to happen this way."

"Amy, no mother ever wants to leave this world after her children. Your mom and dad are waiting in heaven to hold you."

Amy gradually stopped crying. For the next several minutes, she described what she wanted for her memorial service. As Karen held he friend's fragile hand, she wondered how life could have brought them to this sorrowful farewell. Tears streamed down Karen's face when she hugged her best friend goodbye and said, "I love you, Amy."

When Karen walked out, Terry was standing in the garage.

She hugged him and said, "Thank you, Terry for taking such good care of Amy. You and Erica have allowed me to spend such precious time with her the past weeks and months."

"Karen, you've been a great friend to Amy. She would have done the same for you."

With a trembling heart and voice, Karen said, "I know. I am so blessed that Amy has been my best friend forever.

Far Too Much

Journal Entry

July 17, 2009

I spent time with Jill this afternoon. Her eyes reflect the deep sadness she and her sisters feel. They desperately miss their mother and don't know how many days it will be until they lose their sister. Everyone believes Amy is holding on until Erica's birthday party that is still two weeks away. For the first time, Terry sees the look of defeat in Amy's eyes. Leona's death has broken her spirit. She is emotionally drained and told Lisa, "I have no more tears to cry. My tears are all dried up."

All the sisters are spending as much time as they can with her. They sit at the end of the couch and massage her legs to ease the painful swelling of gout that has settled in her knees and ankles. During a private moment together, Amy said, "Lisa, why do you think God has put me through all this my whole life?"

"Amy, you'll probably never know why. Somewhere along the way, you've changed someone's life. You've made people think twice about what they are doing, what they are saying and how they are acting. You've changed Brad's life, and you've changed mine. We are all part of God's plan. Our lives are His and not ours."

Amy listened but didn't respond. She looked away with uncertainty and uneasiness.

Everyone is exhausted with sorrow. Brad is spending a lot of time at the house. He senses when Terry needs his broad shoulder to lean on for support. Brad knows when he needs to take care of Amy in order for Terry to sleep a few hours.

Each day is now a competition between 'life' and 'death.' Amy's heart refuses to give up on her like her lungs have. Although her soul is ready to be with her mom and dad, Amy's heart continues to beat until it has carried her to Erica's birthday party.

My Birthday Party

By Erica Greer

On July 31ˢᵗ, I had my sixteenth birthday party. I had really turned sixteen on July 28ᵗʰ but the 31ˢᵗ was the best night to celebrate so that all my friends and relatives could come. I had invited about forty of my friends and there were nearly twenty family members coming. With so many people, we decided ahead of time to have the party in the garage that my cousin and I had fun decorating.

My mom had been on a ventilator four months, and she had been out of the hospital and home about four months. Even though she could barely get off the couch some days, she was in good spirits. She was just as excited as I was for the party.

My aunts brought all kinds of food and snacks for all the guests who started to arrive at 6 o'clock. After we ate, it was time for the birthday cake. My dad and I wheeled Mom and all her machines into the garage so she could enjoy the party and watch me blow out my candles. After everyone sang "Happy Birthday" to me, I started passing out pieces of cake. Unexpectedly, one of my so-called 'best friends' decided to shove a piece of cake in my face. As their 'best friend,' I felt obligated to return the favor. After I got the cake out of my eyes, I knew this was going to be a memorable night. It was the next morning that I wasn't prepared for at all.

My dad had set up a fire pit in the middle of our driveway, and my friends gathered around it most of the night. We all played a few intense rounds of musical chairs and some water balloon games that I never won. One of my aunts brought a giant beach ball so we girls decided to play a giant version of volleyball.

It started getting dark about 9 o'clock. A lot of us sat around the fire roasting hot dogs, marshmallows and making s'mores. By then, the party had died down. Most of my family left and about half of my other guests were gone. By 11 o'clock, the party was over. Everyone was gone except Karlee and Alyssa. I had invited them to spend the night.

After we finished cleaning up, we went inside. My friends went straight to my bedroom while I told Mom all about the party. Then I gave her a hug and kiss 'goodnight' and said, "I love you, Mom."

My friends and I stayed up until 5 a.m. just talking, laughing and making shadow puppets. Alyssa and I woke up about 8 o'clock in the morning because she needed to leave to go shopping for school clothes. After I walked her out, I went back to bed.

About thirty minutes later, my mom's ventilator machine was beeping nonstop. I jumped out of bed and made my way down the hall to find my dad near my mom's side on the couch. That's when he said, "Erica, it's time."

With a shocked look on my face, I choked out the words, "Are you sure?"

He just looked at me and shook his head 'yes.'

Dad and I started telling Mom we loved her as many times as possible. We tried to comfort her, but as we said, "I love you" one last time, she took her last big breath. That was the day my mother died.

Run, Amy, Run!

Journal Entry

August 1, 2009

Jill called a few minutes ago and said, "Beth, we lost Amy this morning."

As I pictured the slender girl at recess, I picked up my journal and wrote the following tribute that Erica wanted read at her mother's memorial service.

"Run, Amy, Run!"

Each morning when we awaken to a new day, we are given the opportunity to make a choice. We can choose to be grateful by embracing the day, or we can choose to disregard one of God's many blessings. In a sense, living our lives is a metaphor for running a race. We can choose to run with all our might, or we can fall back and watch the other runners pass us by.

Every day of her earthly life, Amy Greer ran the race with conviction and courage. As a young girl, she sprinted through the barnyard with the pure innocence of a child growing up on a farm with four older sisters. She ran with determination as a daughter raised by parents committed to family values and a strong work ethic. When Amy married Terry, she ran with passion. She had found the love of her life, a devoted man who loved, protected and cared for her. Upon the birth of their beautiful daughter, Amy ran with pride and an all-consuming joy that only a mother's heart can feel.

For most of her life, Amy ran the race with a debilitating disease that invaded her lungs. Each time she struggled with her illness, her family and close friends were by her side. They prayed that God would give her the strength to live. He did time and time again. God knew this valiant fighter wanted to stay in the race.

Today, Amy is running a heavenly race and is determined

110

to win. Imagine this scene: Amy is standing at the starting line. The gun sounds. She breaks out quickly and confidently. She is smiling as she passes the other runners. The farther she runs, the faster she runs. She is breathing freely and without pain. Her lungs are pumping energy that will carry her to the finish line.

She can hear her family cheering her on with shouts of "Run, Amy, run!" She can see her mom and dad ahead with outstretched arms to hug her.

As she crosses the finish line, God lifts her up in victory for all to see.

Then Amy asks, "Did I win, God?"

God smiles proudly and answers, "You won, Amy. Your won the race!"

Afterword

In God's Hands

December 2009

Amy loved spending time at the ocean on summer vacations. She looked forward to wearing her sunglasses and sun hat, grabbing her portable oxygen tank and walking to the beach. She delighted in walking along the shore and making footprints in the sand that said, "Amy was here."

Amy wanted to go back to the ocean in her final weeks of life. Terry had everything planned to make her last dream come true. When Amy ran out of time, the two people she treasured most returned to the ocean for her.

As Terry and Erica retraced Amy's footprints, they absorbed every detail. They felt Amy's presence in the grandeur of the ocean and the serenity of the sunset. They were in awe of the brief rainbow that appeared like Amy's messenger to say, "I'm right here beside you."

With tears streaming down her face, Erica gazed at the ocean and said, "Mom, you would love being here today. It's amazing and beautiful."

Erica dropped five white flowers in the water that formed an arc and one red flower that floated to the middle of the celestial formation. Sensing her mother's presence, Erica said, "Mom, you are here. This is your day."

The waves cradled the flowers until the tide slowly carried them out to sea. Terry put his arm around his daughter, the miracle he and Amy created.

"Erica, this is just what Mom wanted."

As more tears fell into the ocean, Terry took a deep, comforting breath. He felt like he was gently handing Amy back to God, her Creator and Protector.

Amy's Embrace

Journal Entry

November 2009

Amy was simply unforgettable. Even as a young girl, she was determined to make the best of things. She chose to live with hope that conquered despair; she chose to embrace those she loved and this love conquered all.

Amy's family and close friends were her life. It would bring her such joy to know they have written her story. Without question, Amy would want their sentiments shared.

Erica: *I don't have any siblings so Mom was really my best friend, my sister, and my mother at the same time. I miss her so much and would give anything to get her back healthy. She always called me her 'miracle baby.' I never got to tell her this, but she was 'my miracle.'*

Terry: *I never knew when Amy and I got married that we'd be able to have nearly twenty years together. We were never expected to have a child and we did. I met her when I was fifteen years old, so Amy was really my soul mate for twenty-four years.*

Brad: *I reminded Amy many times what a privilege it was to help take care of her. If it meant having the chance to live one more day, she tried anything the doctors suggested. Amy wasn't afraid to take the chance to live.*

Jill: *My little sister, Amy was my inspiration in life. Whenever I wasn't feeling well, I'd think of her, get up and move forward with whatever needed to be done. Amy worked hard to breathe every day, while the rest of us took breathing for granted. Whenever her health allowed it, she was 'a doer' and 'a helper.' Amy was also a prankster who loved a practical joke. She would laugh with the rest of us until her coughing would overtake her laughter. I love her and miss her. She will always* *be my inspiration.*

Lisa: *Amy once asked, "Why me, Lisa? Why did God choose me to suffer with cystic fibrosis?" My answer was, "We'll never know why, Amy. We accept God's will and make the best of it." Amy influenced my outlook on life, and I wish everyone would sign his or her driver's license and be an organ donor. Amy's new lungs were a gift of extended time to our family, and we are thankful for the blessings God has bestowed upon us.*

Cathy: *Amy's illness was just that-her illness; it wasn't who she was. Amy was a big smile, a big heart and a big force in all our lives. And now, she's left a big hole in our hearts. We'd be smart if we lived our lives like Amy did.*

Deb: *As Amy's disease progressed and we all grew older, we also grew in our understanding of what Amy's future held. We came to realize and appreciate the many miracles that occurred within her full, short life. Some of these miracles included her mental and physical strength, her husband, her 'miracle' daughter, and the gift of new lungs. There were many other miracles, like her ability to breathe against her body's will, finding just the right doctor at the right time, or someone in the family being able to convince a very strong-willed wife, daughter, and sister when it was time to seek medical help. By her courageous attitude and actions, Amy has made me a better and more compassionate individual. Through all her trials, we have learned as a family that nothing is more important than family. Amy taught us that life is precious and that we need to focus on what is truly important. I love my sister and miss her terribly. We never wanted this time to come, but it has. Now, we must continue to move forward and carry on Amy's legacy by sharing her life with others.*

Audrey: *Aunt Amy always made me laugh. One summer vacation, Amy, Erica and I were swimming in the ocean. We spotted a dolphin, and Amy wanted it to swim closer. She made a hand signal and called for the dolphin. Needless to say, she looked funny attempting to get the dolphin's attention.*

Kelsey: *I though Aunt Amy would win the battle with her disease. In a way, she won the battle every day she lived. She taught me to* *appreciate everything I have like my good health; she also taught me to appreciate my family, especially my mother.*

Devin: *My cousins and I often had a fashion show when the whole family got together every Sunday at Grandma and Grandpa's house. We dressed up in our moms' old prom dresses and other outfits. Amy's red, lacy prom dress was always worn because it was one of the prettiest ones. Everyone laughed while my aunts and grandparents had a good time trying to guess whose outfit we were wearing.*

Blair: *Amy was a wonderful aunt. She always had a positive attitude and was kind to me. Amy was and is the toughest person I know. What a fighter.*

Alyona: *Watching Aunt Amy fight her illness taught me what it takes to be a winner in life. Whenever I compete in sports, I will never give up until the game is over. Amy taught me to fight to the end.*

Maria:

Forever and Always

All the memories with you,
Are sealed in my heart.
Forever and always,
From the very start.
You made us so happy
By being who you are.

And when you left us
You became a star.
I still think about you and
Picture you in my head,
When something good happened,
"I'm proud of you," you said.

I'll always remember everything
We've been through,
So forever and for always
There's a spot in my
Heart just for you!

115

Mike: *I think of Amy and her struggles every day. I never once heard my sister-in-law say how badly she felt. I've promised myself that I will never complain about my health or anything. I hope that Amy, Leona, Bob and my dad are sharing a good laugh in heaven today.*

Brad: *Amy did not make others feel sorry for her. My sister-in-law participated in life by taking her fistful of pills each meal, poking herself for sugar tests and giving herself insulin injections when needed. Amy understood better than most of us that time is finite, and that every day is a gift from God.*

Karen: *Amy was more like a sister to me than a friend. After Amy died, I was so grateful that Terry invited me to join the family for the private viewing. It gave me closure for my dearest friend. Amy looked beautiful and peaceful. A friend like Amy only comes around once in your life.*

Jayme: *I had the privilege of seeing my friend a week before she left us. I knew I needed to see Amy and say goodbye. I wanted her to know I loved her. Our visit was short, and I left with my heart breaking for Terry and Erica. When we lose a loved one, we are forced to recognize the frailty of life and the lack of our control. We take comfort in accepting that a loving God cares for us and is in complete control.*

Heather: *The last time I saw Amy was at our 20th high school reunion. Even though I didn't live in the area any longer, we stayed in touch. I always felt a connection with her because two of my children went through some difficult medical issues and spent a lot of time in the hospital. Amy sent me a card and said she was thinking of me during that time. She gave me a picture of Erica at the reunion. I felt honored and keep the picture on my refrigerator. It reminds me of Amy and the fun, memorable times we shared.*

Throughout Amy's illness and after her death, Erica was surrounded by supportive friends. They considered Amy their second mom. Erica spoke from her heart when she said, "I depend on my friends so much, and they're always there for me. However low I feel, they make me laugh. Mom and Dad loved having them hang out here. They're like my family.

116

Patrick: When Amy came home from Ann Arbor, she was on the couch hooked to the ventilator. She was watching a show about Michael Jackson with Erica and me. Amy started singing along to the song "Ebony and Ivory" and Erica and I cracked up laughing because she knew all the words. When I left that night, Amy said, "Thank you, Patrick." I knew what she was saying. She appreciated my friendship with Erica. I admired Amy so much. She never gave up.

Monique: I stayed with Erica one week when Terry was in Ann Arbor with Amy. We had a lot of time to talk. I know my faith in God grew stronger in knowing what Amy went through. I asked for people in our church to pray for Amy and her family. She was a beautiful person. I felt comfortable telling her anything. When her mother died, Paige and I brought over a casserole. Amy looked so sad without her mom. I'll never forget the look in her eyes when she thanked us for bringing the food. It was an honor to know Amy.

Alyssa: One of the many things I respected about Amy was how special she made people feel. When she asked me how my day had gone, I knew she really cared. She never judged others. I learned so much watching how Amy lived. She became so frustrated when she went shopping with us and had to carry her portable oxygen tank. Even though she tired easily and needed to sit on the benches when she became winded, she kept going. Amy has made me think twice about the blessings in my life. She taught me how important it is to appreciate my friends and family.

Karlee: When Erica and I were freshmen, I traveled with her family to North Carolina for a wedding. I felt so at ease being with them. I thought it was neat watching how much Erica enjoyed being with her parents. When Amy was in Ann Arbor, I went to visit her. I wasn't afraid when I saw her, but I felt nervous. I kept telling myself that she had made it this far and could pull through again. My faith is much stronger because of Amy. I know God helped her live as long as she did. Terry took a picture of Erica and Amy the day I was there. Erica was in Amy's bed with her and they were smiling. I had the picture framed and gave it to Erica at Amy's funeral.

The bottom of the silver picture from Karlee was engraved with these words:

Mom

A life well-lived,
A heart well-loved,
We'll miss you always.

November 29, 1968—August 1, 2009

When Amy was in the hospital on Mother's Day in May, 2007, Erica and Terry drove to Ann Arbor to personally deliver their Mother's Day cards. Amy later wrote these notes inside their cards:

Erica stayed with me in the hospital from Saturday night through Sunday. It was Mother's Day, and it meant so much to me that she was here. We had a great night and a good 'Mother's Day' the next day. I love her so much. She is my world. Terry and Erica brought me flowers and a new outfit. We had dinner from a nice restaurant.
I love those two!

Dear Amy

Journal Entry

March 2010

Dear Amy,

The last letter I wrote to you was at the end of your eighth grade year. That was nearly 27 years ago. The intent of that letter was to thank you for touching my life and teaching me the true definition of courage. Throughout my teaching career, I had hundreds of students whom I enjoyed. You, however, were the most inspirational.

This letter is to thank you once again. This time, you have more than touched my life. You have changed it. I have had the privilege to write the story of your heroic journey, one that you wanted to share in order to help others struggling with cystic fibrosis.

Writing your story has been a beautiful labor of love, especially from Terry, Erica, your sisters, Brad, and Karen. Writing your story has also been an emotional labor of love. Each time we met, many tears were shed. Our mission, though, was to work through the tears and honor you, Amy, by writing a book that promoted awareness for your two passions: continued cystic fibrosis research and increased awareness for people to become organ donors.

I went to the license bureau today to renew my driver's license. As I was searching through my purse, the lady behind the counter began asking a series of quick questions that required a simple 'yes' or 'no' answer. When she asked if I would like to be an organ donor, I spontaneously said, "Yes! I definitely want to be an organ donor. My friend was able to spend many more years with her family because some donor gave her new lungs."

People were in line behind me and beside me. I know they heard me. As I left the building, I thought of you. I hope that my

119

outburst made someone think twice about becoming a donor.

On the way home, I drove by an elementary playground where young students were jumping rope and playing games of tag at recess. I thought of you again. I wondered if any of them endure days when they can't breathe freely.

Amy, I pray that your story will touch many lives. I pray that your story will encourage people to become organ donors. Due to physical limitations, there are other slender girls who are struggling to win the race at recess. I pray that many donors' lungs will one day enable them 'to live with all their might' like you did. Your spirit lives on in everyone you loved, Amy. Your spirit lives on in everyone whose lives you touched and changed.

With love and admiration,
Beth Huffman